THE JOURNAL JUNKIES WORKSHOP

visual ammunition for the art addict

NORTH LIGHT BOOKS

North Light Books
CINCINNATI, OHIO

to the image — image
we inhabit. saturated cul...

FACe

What do I really see?

What do I truly see?

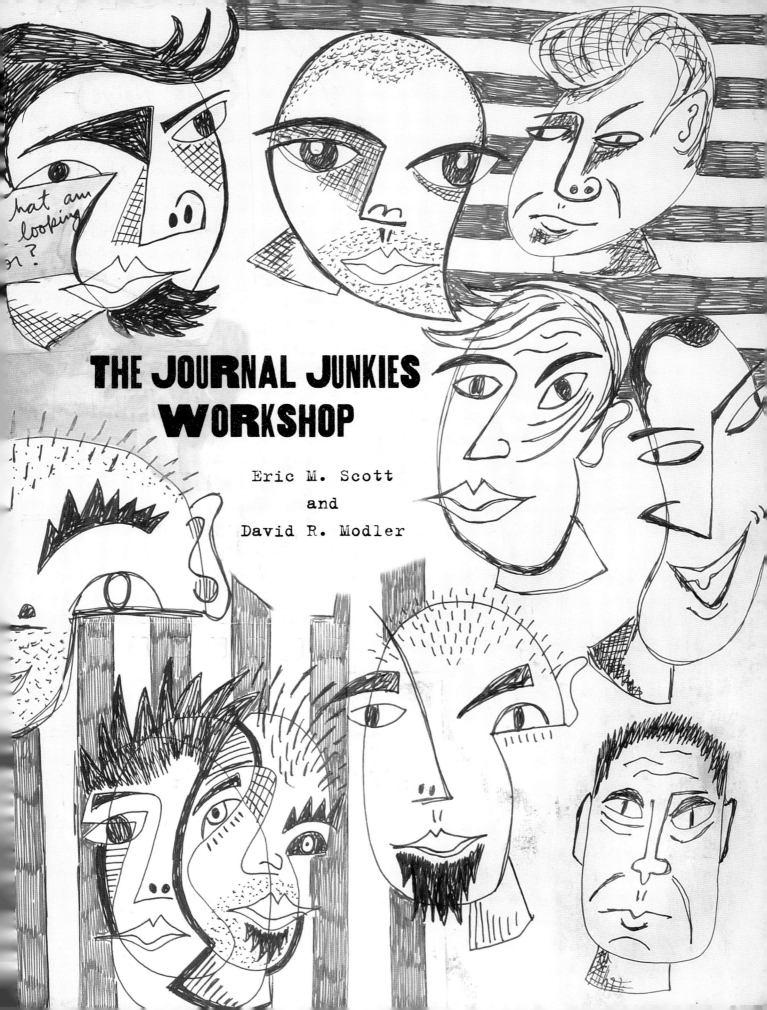

THE JOURNAL JUNKIES
WORKSHOP

Eric M. Scott

and

David R. Modler

14 13 12 11   5 4

Distributed in Canada by Fraser Direct
100 Armstrong Avenue
Georgetown, ON, Canada L7G 5S4
Tel: (905) 877-4411

Distributed in the U.K. and Europe by David
& Charles
Brunel House, Newton Abbot, Devon, TQ12
4PU, England
Tel: (+44) 1626 323200, Fax: (+44) 1626
323319
Email: postmaster@davidandcharles.co.uk

Distributed in Australia by Capricorn Link
P.O. Box 704, S. Windsor NSW, 2756
Australia
Tel: (02) 4577-3555

Library of Congress Cataloging in
Publication Data
Scott, Eric M.
  The journal junkies workshop : visual
ammunition for the art addict / Eric M. Scott
and David R. Modler.
    p. cm.
  Includes index.
  ISBN-13: 978-1-60061-456-9 (pbk. : alk.
paper)
  ISBN-10: 1-60061-456-6 (pbk. : alk. paper)
  1. Handicraft. 2. Scrapbook journaling. I.
Modler, David R., II. Title.
  TT157.S337 2010
  745.593--dc22

2009039834

Editor **Liz Casler**
Designer **Kelly O'Dell**
Production Coordinator
Greg Nock
Photographers
Christine Polomsky &
Al Parrish

fw
media
www.fwmedia.com

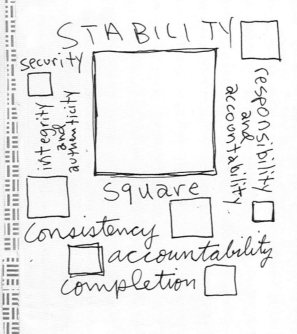

SIGNS OF LIFE
the five universal shapes
and how to use them solidity

STABILITY
security
integrity and authenticity
responsibility and accountability
square
consistency
accountability
completion

Balancing
connectio
relation
collabor

METRIC CONVERSION CHART		
To convert	*to*	*multiply by*
Inches	Centimeters	2.54
Centimeters	Inches	0.4
Feet	Centimeters	30.5
Centimeters	Feet	0.03
Yards	Meters	0.9
Meters	Yards	1.1

...it saves lives ... it's going to change the world

daniel h. pink

A WHOLE NEW MIND

ACKNOWLEDGMENTS

We would like to thank those at F+W Media and North Light Books who had a hand in the publishing of this book. We would like to thank acquisitions editor Tonia Davenport for her initial interest in our idea and guidance through the proposal process. We would like to thank editor Liz Casler for all of her hard work and walking us through the shaping and publication of the book. We would like to thank photographer Christine Polomsky for her fabulous photos, sense of humor and love of great music. We would like to thank designer Kelly O'Dell for her unique look and feel in the design of the book.

We also would like to thank everyone who has ever come to one of our presentations, workshops or seminars. Sharing the journal has been important to us, and the amazing feedback from these experiences led us to want to publish this book in the first place.

Most important, we want to thank Dan Eldon and his family. We feel a kinship with Dan, and we are grateful to his family for bringing his story to light. Dan was the impetus that brought us to this point, and he has inspired us to document our lives and our own personal journeys in this world. Dan is truly at the heart of all this, and we are grateful to him, his mother, Kathy, his father, Mike, and his sister, Amy, for sharing his legacy. Without the journals of Dan Eldon, there would be no Journal Fodder Junkies.

DEDICATION

Dan Eldon

- IT MUST WORK
- LOOK AND FEEL

Eric would like to dedicate this book to Joanne for all of her love, support and understanding.

David would like to dedicate this book to the faculty and staff at the North Carolina Center for the Advancement of Teaching for their support and encouragement of his scholarship and teaching practice.

Together we would like to dedicate this book to the memory of Dan Eldon.

bauhausesque

AND HIGH TOUCH MORE IMPORTANT THAN HIGH TECH

FORM FOLLOWS

Kathy Eldon

In a time of impermanence, when Twitter, iChat and Facebook have replaced letter writing, perhaps the best way to preserve our own history is through journals. Not the stiff, staid diaries our ancestors kept, but living, breathing books filled with photos, writings and artifacts that reflect our lives as they are now—and more important, our dreams for what might be.

As a former art teacher, I started our children on journals when they were very little, bringing along crayons, markers and scrapbooks when our family moved from London to Nairobi, so that Dan, age seven, and Amy, four, could draw their experiences

FOREWORD

in Kenya. Dan covered his book in zebra wrapping paper and recorded his safaris to game parks, sailing expeditions on the Indian Ocean and explorations of the exotic island of Lamu. As he grew older, Dan preferred black artists journals to capture memories of our family trips to Israel, Egypt, South Africa, Brazil and India. He also recorded his adventures in Deziree, his ancient Land Rover, that took him across Africa, living what he called "safari as a way of life."

I was fascinated to see how Dan's journals evolved with his exposure to new cultures, artists and ideas. His books grew fatter as he added doodles and drawings, clippings torn from newspapers and magazines and then decorated them with splashes of ink or acrylic paint. Dan began to layer the pages like an archaeological dig, adding coins and feathers, snippets of snakeskin or swatches of cloth or leather. He interspersed the artifacts with quotations from poetry or songs, along with whimsical comments about girls, school and life. Although he let Amy share his books with special people, he was careful to ink over sections he didn't want anyone else to read and glued scraps of paper over private writings or drawings.

When Dan was nineteen, he led a group of fifteen students across Africa to deliver aid to a refugee camp in Somalia and carefully documented his adventures, including a love triangle involving his best friend. At twenty-one, he traveled to Somalia to document a little-known famine for Reuters News Agency. Dan returned again and again to the war-torn country as a photojournalist and added the horrific images to his growing collection of black books. However, on July 12, 1993, his life was cut short when he and four colleagues were stoned to death by an angry mob. He was twenty-two.

Over the next few years, I discovered nearly twenty of Dan's journals in suitcases, closets, cupboards and garages, waiting for their owner's return. When I mustered the courage to go through them, I began to understand Dan's perception of the world—as well as his vision for a future that was never to be. Chronicle Books published the first collection of Dan's journals, entitled *The Journey Is the Destination*, in 1997, followed by *Dan Eldon, the Art of Life* by Jennifer New. A new book for teens, *Dan Eldon, Life as a Safari*, also published by Chronicle, will accompany a feature film about his life.

I am grateful to David Modler and Eric Scott for *The Journal Junkies Workshop,* which offers every possible tool and resource—ammunition—for anyone wishing to create a journal. Originally inspired by Dan's pages, this book goes far beyond his wildest imagination, using ideas and techniques that reflect the authors' addiction to the art of journal making. It's a brilliant book, one that will transform the lives of journal-makers everywhere.

As you begin to record your life's journey—what Dan would have called your "safari"—please reflect on whether you are living authentically, doing all that you can to fulfill your potential, both for yourself and for the world. After all, as Dan scribbled in the margin of a journal page, the journey is the destination.

KATHY ELDON

For more on Dan Eldon and the foundation he inspired, please visit www.daneldon.org and www.creativevisions.org.

self revelation

TURMOIL

EXHAUSTED

dreamer

THE DAY

indifferent.

MANIFESTOS

full of living

DEEP 8

TABLE OF CONTENTS

TYPES OF FAILURE

ACCIDENT
MISTAKE
WEAKNES
INABILITY
INCORRECT M
USELESSNES
INCOMPATIB
EMBARRASS
CONFUSION
REDUNDAN
OBSOLESCEN
INCOHEREN
UNRECOGNIZ
ABSURDITY
INVISIBILIT
IMPEMANE
DECAY
INSTABILI
FORGETABIL
TARDINESS
DISAPPEAR
CATASTR
UNCERTA
DOUBT
FEAR
DISTRA

We are just two of many people who have been inspired by the life and journals of Dan Eldon. We have spent countless hours poring over the pages of *The Journey Is the Destination,* soaking in their richness and vitality. We have come away with a lot from Dan's journals and have applied those ideas to our own art and lives.

Over the past eleven years as artists and educators, we have been working on the art-making process and its effect on the creation of a unique artifact that we call the visual journal. Along the way, countless artists and educators have inspired us, and we in turn have tried to inspire others. Through the strong friendship the two of us share, we have collaborated, experimented

INTRODUCTION

and encouraged each other to continually grow through our individual studio practices.

Over the years, we have offered countless workshops and presentations on the local, state and national levels where we have invited others to join us in the visual journal experience. We see a need for our media in the artistic realm, as well as the education community. We freely share our passion, our ideas and our motivations. This desire to openly share has led us to put our thoughts into a comprehensive form; that is, the book you now hold in your hands.

We hope to inspire and motivate others, and perhaps bring a few more Journal Junkies along for the ride. Welcome to our world. We hope you enjoy the journey.

DAVID R. MODLER
ERIC M. SCOTT

Emily told me today that she got seve
of her cousins into the journals and
in turn got several friends into the
Slowly the revolution is spreading. F
told me that she was going into
drawal because she had left her
at school over the weekend. Stories
make me aware of how powerful the
is. As I began to retype the journ
book today, I realized how excited
makes me to think that one day
may pick up my book and read
words and find inspiration from
the way I have found inspiration
others. I hope that the book Da
and I are putting together becom
one of those standards that visu-
journalists keep on their shelves. I
been throwing around the idea of th
Journal Fodder Junkies as a business
a website, books, stickers. Dave and I
about it, but I think we both wou
it to come to pass. With contacts Dav
made we are consistently doing works!
NCAT is going to fly for the 3

THE MISSION
who are we?

We are the Journal Fodder Junkies, a phrase Dave coined when we first began offering workshops and presentations for others out there like us—visual artists who have boxes and boxes of stuff waiting to be used in the making of art. When we discovered the visual journal, we discovered a place for all that stuff—what we call fodder. The word *fodder* refers to the coarse, dry food fed to livestock. We use it to refer to all the random ephemera that gets glued into the visual journal. It is food for the journal. The moniker Journal Fodder Junkies has stuck, and we consider it our mission to spread the addictive experience of the visual journal.

ONCE YOU ACCEPT AN IDEA IT'S AN IDEA WHOSE TIME HAS COME.

WANTED
#06281968
DAVID R. MODLER

WANTED
#12221973
ERIC M. SCOTT

RTISTIC ACCOMPLICES

ARTISTIC ACCOMPLICES
February 18 - March 15, 2005
Recent mixed media paintings by David R. Modler and Eric M. Scott

Perquimans Arts League Gallery
Hertford, North Carolina

Opening Reception:
Friday, February 18, 2005 6-8pm

how do you use this book?

Let us first say that the techniques and ideas in this book are by no means all-encompassing or the one and only way to work in the visual journal.

finding your voice is not in jargon

Many techniques, ideas and concepts that others use are not covered here. The tools presented in this book are simply the armaments we employ, and we hope you find them valuable. Each individual must discover for himself what the journal needs to be and how to use it. So be forewarned—this is not a recipe book. We are not going to give you projects, prompts and step-by-step directions for creating certain types of pages from start to finish. Instead, we intend to bombard you with ideas, techniques and suggestions while allowing your creativity to take hold. We will share the basic how-tos with you, but it is up to you as the visual journalist to decide how and when to use those concepts and techniques. We want to foster your creativity. We want to give you the inspiration and the know-how that allows you to find your own path, your own voice, your own style, through the journal. We want you to get caught up in the process and to explore the possibilities. We are here to help you along and offer guidance. So grab a journal and some pens, pencils, markers, paint and fodder, and join us to create your own unique and personal pages.

NAEA Chicago '06

ERIC SCOTT

Name

STONE BRIDGE HIGH SCHOOL VA

what is a visual journal and who keeps one?

That is a good question, and to be honest, our definition changes frequently. The visual journal has many aliases: artist journal, visual thinking journal, artist sketchbook, resource workbook, illuminated journal, interactive notebook and more. Whatever the name, the visual journal is much more than a traditional sketchbook. The traditional sketchbook tends to emphasize drawing and sketching in preparation for larger artwork. The visual journal can do this as well, but it can also become a work of art itself. It is also much more than a traditional journal, which tends to emphasize the recording of events and thoughts in written form. The visual journal combines the visual with the written, the image with the word. You do not need to identify yourself as an artist or writer to keep a visual journal. All you need is the desire to explore your creativity and your inner world and to try something new. The visual journal becomes a rich and layered record of your life that uses words, colors, images and more. The journal becomes whatever it needs to be.

A visual journal is unique to its creator, and different people keep one for different reasons. Some use the journal as a way to observe and illustrate their environment, others as a document of their lives or as a record of travel. For every journal-keeper, the visual journal is a unique and personal expression that evolves over time. No two people approach the journal in the exact same way. Each visual journalist must find his or her own voice—his or her own journey—in order for the journal to become personally relevant and important. In the following pages, we explore ideas, techniques and concepts that can help visual journalists of all experiences and skill levels create rich and exuberant personal pages.

There is no one right way to keep a visual journal. Every visual journalist must find his or her own way through the journal, discovering the techniques and methods that work best. Whatever the methods, the visual journal is a remarkable place for self-expression and self-discovery. You simply need to be open to the process.

We will get into some of the how-tos later. For us, the journaling process is a nonlinear process. We do not complete one page and move on to the next. Instead, we begin a lot of pages using paint, collage, drawing and words, and then we return to rework and add to pages already in progress. Sometimes we go back months later to pages that seem to be missing something and add new elements. Sometimes we find a piece of fodder that just needs to go on a certain page, or a solution to a troubling page will present itself as we work on another. In a way, the journal is never finished. It is always in a state of becoming. However, that is our particular approach, and many other people approach the visual journal in a linear manner. Some use the visual journal as a daily journal to express their thoughts, feelings and daily experiences within the pages. What's important is to work in the journal in a manner that is productive and comfortable for you.

One thing that remains consistent for us is that we try to use our journals every day, even if only for five minutes. We both use the journal in our studios as one aspect of our art, but most often we use the journal when we are away from the studio. Although having hours of uninterrupted time to work in the journal is a luxury, more often than not it is the spaces of ten or fifteen minutes in a coffee shop or watching television that add up to the rich, visual artifact that is the journal. The journal is a habit we have cultivated over the years. It is a creative connection to the studio and to ourselves.

CAN ART
BE UGLY?

OBJECTIVES

The visual journal can serve several purposes. For many people, it is part sketchbook, part diary, part notebook, part dream journal, part daily planner, part to-do list, part doodle pad and part trash heap. Whatever the purpose the journalist has in mind, one thing is constant—the visual journal transcends words and transcends simple image by melding words and visual references. This melding of written vocabulary with visual vocabulary makes the visual journal truly special and powerful. Often when words fail, we can best express ourselves through color, line, shapes and images, and when we cannot find the right images, words can take over and express our thoughts, feelings and ideas. The visual journal is a record of our lives with all the experiences and memories thrown into one ever-expanding document.

an eveRything book

For us, the visual journal is truly an everything book. We have many reasons for keeping our visual journals, and they tend to serve different purposes at different times. We find that our journals are an extension of ourselves and that they become a valuable piece of documentation for our lives. The visual journal is an extension of the studio—a place to take notes; a place to keep track of dates, places and things; a place to sort out our lives, our feelings and our thoughts; and a place to create personal meaning. It is a personal as well as a profes- sional tool, and when you look through our journals, you are just as likely to find daily reminders and notes from meetings as you are to find personal artwork and self-reflection. Some people develop themes for their journals, and some keep separate journals for different aspects of their lives.

a Reflective Space

The visual journal is a reflective space that can affect and change people's lives as they get in touch with their inner selves. It is not uncommon for people to become addicted to the visual journal, to tote it everywhere and to work in it at any opportunity, and so it becomes an invaluable tool for life, helping individuals explore feelings, issues, ideas, materials, techniques and images. It is a vehicle by which to expand one's understanding and knowledge of the world and of one's place in it. The innermost thoughts and ideas expressed in the journal speak as a true extension of its creator. The visual journal is a place to expose one's true self to the light of day, and because of this personal nature, true meaning and purpose can open up as the world and experiences are translated into concrete, visual form. It is a place that is unique to the individual—a place where one's creativity can blossom and grow—a place with one rule: DO!

PROCESS

65

- a proceeding or moving forward
- the course of being done
- course, as of time
- a continuing development involving many changes

163 - a particular method of doing something, generally involving a number of steps or operations

MODUS

Procedure
Proceeding
course
act
motion
step
measure

operation
functioning
action
performance
exercise
play
work
working
working
function
office
agency
management
conduct
running
driving
steering
handling
manipulation

OPERANDI
655

way   order
wise   lines
manner   line
means   line of action
mode   modus operandi (L.)
form   mode of procedure
fashion   the way of
style   the how
cut
tone
guise
method
system
usage
procedure
course
practice

Modus Operandi
manner of operating
the way or method of doing or making

THE MUNITIONS DUMP

Hopefully you are itching to get under way. However, if you are not familiar with the visual journal or some of the basic art materials used to engage in one, you may be wondering how to begin. Some information follows about journals and art media to give you some things to think about as you begin your adventure. You definitely do not need to rush out and spend hundreds of dollars on journals and materials. Often people can find the basic materials and equipment they need to get started around the house. For those already familiar with the journal and the materials, the information here may tip you off to some things that you hadn't thought about before. If you already have a journal and some art materials and you want to jump right in, skip to Section Two.

THE JOURNAL

Where does the visual journalist start? First you need a vessel—something to contain all of your visual and written expressions. Journals come in all shapes and sizes—from the cheap and mass-produced to the expensive and handcrafted. A journal can be anything from a spiral-bound notebook to an artist's sketchbook to an altered book. The selection of a journal is a completely personal choice. Some visual journalists invest in only a certain size and particular brand. Others jump from form to form, depending on their current whim. You will want a book that you feel comfortable using and one that fits your needs and intentions.

Size

Portability is a factor when considering size. Should your journal fit easily in a purse or briefcase or bag? Should you tote it under your arm? Or should its size be something in between? Size does matter! Large artist sketchbooks intimidate some newbies, and other artists feel confined by the smaller journals that line bookstore shelves. You want a journal that fits you—one with which you are comfortable and will easily and consistently use.

Paper

There are trade-offs when it comes to paper type and quality. You will need to consider how you plan on using the journal when considering the type of paper. Should the paper be lined or unlined? Many artists prefer unlined paper, but that can be problematic for someone used to traditional journals. Should the paper be thick or thin? If the paper is too thin, it can tear easily, and materials such as marker and paint easily bleed through. Yet thin paper makes the journal less expensive. Thick papers such as watercolor paper provide a tough surface on which to work, and bleeding and tearing are held to a minimum. Watercolor paper is ideal for use with multiple media—everything from collage to drawing to painting. Yet these journals often have fewer pages and tend to be more expensive. A heavy drawing paper is also good for multiple media, but you may encounter some bleeding and tearing.

binding

Journals and sketchbooks come with many different bindings. Simple softcover bindings are usually inexpensive but have a tendency to fall apart easily. More expensive journals often have stronger bindings and are less likely to fall apart. Hardbound journals have a more durable cover, but you may still have to reinforce the binding if you add a lot of collage and fodder to your journal. Spiral bindings take up less space when opened and allow for some expandability when adding collage to the journal.

Some visual journalists prefer to hand bind their own journals, thereby controlling every aspect of the book. Teaching the skills required for such an undertaking lies outside the scope of this book, but many wonderful resources exist if you want to bind your own journal.

cost

All the above factors play a part in the cost of a journal. You may feel inhibited by an exquisite and expensive hand-bound book, fearing pressure to do something worthy of such a precious format. A less expensive book may make you more willing to experiment. If uncertain, choose a moderately priced book of medium size with decent paper until you gain confidence and fully discover your path and needs. Often you need to experiment a bit to find the format that suits your needs and nature. Again, the choice needs to be one with which you are comfortable and one that you will use consistently. We prefer 11" × 14" (28cm × 36cm) hardbound artist sketchbooks that are moderately priced, with 65- or 70-lb. (135gsm or 150 gsm) paper capable of supporting a wide range of media.

A RTIST SUPPLIES AND MEDIA

The traditional journal or sketchbook relies on a single basic writing or drawing medium, but the ability to use any and all materials or media in the visual journal helps you to take it up a level. Art supplies, like journals, come in a range of qualities and prices. As a general rule, experiment with a little quantity before shelling out big bucks for the best quality. Sometimes less expensive materials suit the needs of an individual. Here recommendations follow about what to consider when delving into the artistic side of the visual journal. Remember that you certainly do not need all of these materials and some materials, you want to use are probably excluded. Consider this a simple overview of some of the possibilities.

dRawing and wRiting media

Drawing and writing tools are some of the most readily available materials and tend to be the most portable. You can find pens, pencils, markers, colored pencils and crayons in any office supply store or home office section of your neighborhood general store. Many visual journalists quickly find a particular pen, pencil or marker that becomes a favorite.

Pens

There are a few things to consider when deciding on the right pen for a given situation. There are ballpoint, roller ball, flair tip, metallic and gel pens, so take time to explore the various options with their various inks. It is always a good idea to have a variety of colors and types on hand.

Because of their opaque ink, gel and metallic pens can create interesting effects and often are good for use on top of darker colors. Roller ball and ballpoint pens are versatile pens good for writing and drawing. A waterproof pen is invaluable if you are using a lot of wet media because you can safely paint water-based media over waterproof and water-resistant ink with little or no bleeding. However, bleeding can have an interesting and desirable effect.

Pencils

Graphite pencils come in a full range of shade values so you can achieve various degrees of lightness and darkness fairly easily. Pencils are graded by hardness, with 8B being one of the softest and 8H being one of the hardest. The softer the pencil, the more heavily the graphite can be applied. With harder pencils, lighter values are easier to achieve. The standard No. 2 pencil falls in the middle of this range and is extremely versatile for writing and drawing. It's always good to have a few different graphite pencils on hand, especially if you get into shading and working with value.

Water-soluble graphite pencils, when used on plain dry paper, look and act like regular pencils. But brush water over your marks and you get some amazing painterly effects. Once dry, they have a watercolor look to them. These pencils are similar to watercolor pencils.

Markers

Markers tend to be inexpensive yet are an effective way to add color to your journal. They come in bright colors and a variety of sizes and are widely available. There are two basic types: water-based and solvent-based. Water-based markers are also known as watercolor markers and often are associated with children's art supplies. You can find them in a variety of places, such as your local drugstore, grocery or office supply store. You can achieve painterly effects by brushing water over the marks you make, just as you can with water-soluble graphite pencils. You can also use these markers effectively with watercolor pencils (more on that in Section Two). Water-based markers come in a variety of colors with varying tips and sizes. Because they are water-based and transparent, they bleed when wet and do not write well on glossy or dark surfaces.

Solvent-based markers include permanent markers, fine art markers and paint markers. Water does not affect the ink of most solvent-based markers. They can have a strong odor and bleed easily through light- and medium-weight paper. Permanent markers are widely available and come in a huge range of colors. Their ink tends to be transparent—not crystal clear like a pane of glass, but transparent enough to see what is underneath. Only dark colors allow good coverage on surfaces other than white paper. Another type of solvent-based marker is the paint marker. Paint markers come in a variety of opaque colors, particularly metallic colors, and must be shaken before use. Because they are opaque, they write well on most surfaces and work well on dark background colors and glossy surfaces.

Colored Pencil

Colored pencils are another effective way to add color to your journal. They come in a large variety of colors, but a basic set of twelve is a good start. You can use colored pencils like regular pencils and can shade from dark to light depending upon the amount of pressure you apply. By applying more pressure, rich and bright colors can be achieved. Colored pencils are used most effectively when colors are mixed and blended. This occurs directly on the paper as you layer and overlap colors—of course, blendability is affected by the quality of colored pencil used. When used this way, a simple set of twelve colored pencils can give you an almost infinite color palette.

Colored pencils also come in a water-soluble form, better known as watercolor pencil. These pencils can be used with water and wet media to create different effects (more on that in Section Two). Because of their versatility and portability, watercolor pencils are a favorite of the Journal Fodder Junkies.

Crayon

Crayons are usually thought of as a child's medium, and often when a box is given to an adult, an amazing thing happens. All of a sudden, the adult is a five-year-old again. Sometimes this is what we need—to take joy in the simple act of making marks like a child. But crayons can be mixed and blended on the paper with complex results, too. Don't be afraid of a child's medium. Some interesting things can happen when you open your mind to crayons.

Crayons also come in water-soluble form and work very much like watercolor pencils and water-soluble graphite. Because of their broad shape, water-soluble crayons are useful for covering large areas quickly. Most arts and crafts stores sell water-soluble crayons.

wet media

Along with the water-soluble media mentioned previously, different types of paints are suitable for use in the journal. You can use watercolor and acrylic paints to cover large areas and create rich layers. Watercolors, gouache and acrylic paints can all be found in arts and crafts stores.

Watercolor Paint

Watercolor paint is probably one of the easiest ways to add color to the journal, but because of its unpredictability, it can also be one of the most frustrating. Watercolor paint can be hard to control, but with a little practice, it yields rewarding results.

Watercolor is a transparent medium. You can control the strength of the colors you paint by adjusting the amount of water you use. The more water, the lighter and less intense the color will be.

Watercolor usually comes in tubes or pans (cakes). Watercolor tubes contain a concentrated liquid watercolor and are most often associated with the fine arts. Because of the concentration, a little paint goes a long way. The watercolor paint that comes in tubes tends to be of a higher quality than that in pans, comes in a wider variety of colors and costs more.

Many people associate pans of watercolor with kids painting. These semimoist cakes of watercolor come in trays, and you activate the paints with a wet brush. Though somewhat more limited in color and quality than tubes, watercolor pans can still yield rich and pleasant results.

Gouache, an opaque or semiopaque watercolor paint, comes in tubes or small jars. Its opacity allows you to use it on top of darker background colors than other types of watercolor paint allow. This makes for interesting layering possibilities. Gouache is considered a fine art medium and is more expensive than other watercolor paints.

Acrylic Paint

Acrylic is a thick, polymer-based paint that comes in tubes, bottles or jars and a full range of colors. Colors vary from the very opaque to the very transparent. Acrylic makes a good paint on which to layer other materials because when acrylic dries, it resembles plastic and is very durable. You can easily thin acrylic paints with water. However, unlike watercolor and gouache, once acrylic paint has dried, it no longer bleeds, even if you put water on it.

Many mixed-media artists favor acrylic paint because when used in thin layers, it dries quickly. Be aware that thicker layers of paint tend to take longer to dry. You can easily clean wet acrylic paint with warm water and soap, making it suitable for your journal. However, if you leave acrylic paint to dry on your brushes, it can ruin them. To use acrylic paints, you need a palette, a brush and a container of water, and that makes acrylic more suitable to the studio than the travel bag.

adhesives

The right adhesive is essential for gluing in all the bits and pieces the visual journalist collects and incorporates into the journal. It is important that the ephemera that make your journal so rich stay attached and do not fall out. Some people use a variety of tapes to secure items in their journals, but we find that glues tend to give a cleaner look and last longer. Of course, it's important to remember that all adhesives can deteriorate over time.

Glues

When selecting a glue product, you must consider both the material you intend to adhere and the surface to which you intend to adhere it. Most glues work best on porous surfaces. We consider glue sticks, book-binding paste and acrylic gel medium three of the best glues for use in journals.

A good quality glue stick is a vital component of the basic journal kit. Glue sticks can adhere everything from thick cardstock to thin paper into the journal. Because of their low moisture content, glue sticks do not wrinkle or bubble papers the way white liquid glue does. Their screw caps make them perfect for a travel kit. Some people have difficulty with glue sticks simply because they do not spread enough of the adhesive on the back of collage material, but this problem is easily overcome with ample application.

Book-binding paste is a thick paste that you spread with a stiff paintbrush. It works with a variety of materials, including those that are thick or slick. Book-binding paste lends itself more to work done in the studio than to a travel kit because of the need for a brush.

Gel medium is a clear acrylic product meant to be mixed into acrylic paint, but you can use it as a very effective adhesive on its own. Gel medium tends to be thicker than an acrylic gloss or matte medium, making it good for holding collage materials flat. Because acrylic paint is nonporous, glue sticks do not adhere well to it, but because gel medium is itself acrylic, it adheres very well.

Tape

Tape provides a quick and easy way to adhere items in your journal. You can use any type of tape, but be aware that many types deteriorate over time, becoming brittle and losing adhesion. Transparent and masking tapes tend to be the most common, but packaging tape is valuable for its use in effective image transfers as well as its adhesive qualities (see Section Two). It's always good to have several kinds of tape around, and often they come in handy for their aesthetic and decorative qualities.

equipment

Below you will find a list of a variety of equipment and tools you may want to consider using. You will find many of these items in your home; others you may need to purchase at an office supply or hardware store. You will find these articles invaluable as you begin to explore possibilities with art materials.

Brushes

In order to use your paints and water-soluble materials, you will need a variety of brushes. Consider getting several soft-bristle acrylic brushes in various sizes as well as several watercolor brushes. Larger brushes work better for creating wash effects and covering expansive areas in your journal. Smaller brushes work better for creating detail work. Soft-bristle brushes are great for smooth paint application, and coarse-bristle brushes are good when you want to scrub the surface a bit.

Mixing Tray or Palette

A mixing tray or palette for paint is vital, but you don't need to spend a lot of money on it. You can use an old plate or an inexpensive plastic artist palette.

Water Cups

You'll need water cups for rinsing brushes and adding water to water-based media. Old plastic cups make great water cups, as do large plastic jars. You probably should not use your favorite cup because it will get dingy after a while.

Scissors

A good pair of scissors is a must, and a small pair is convenient for a travel kit.

Craft Knife

Although not essential, a craft knife can come in handy for making cutouts in pages and cutting straight lines with the help of a metal ruler.

Cutting Mat

It's good to have a self-healing cutting mat for use with a craft knife to avoid unwanted cuts into work surfaces or underlying pages. You can use a piece of cardboard for this as well.

Burnisher

You can use a burnisher to press materials flat as well as for certain image transfer processes (more on that in Section Two). An old, flat wooden or metal spoon can be an effective burnisher, as can a flat paint scraper. You can use bone folders for both folding paper and burnishing.

Stencils/Lettering Guides

Stencils provide an easy way to add lettering and shapes to your journal. Thin, flexible stencils are widely available and very portable. You can use stencils with many different media. Plastic stencils in particular are durable and easily cleaned.

Rubber Stamps and Hand-Carved Stamps

Using rubber stamps and ink pads or paint, you can quickly and effectively add images and letters to pages. Carve your own stamps from vinyl erasers or corks using a craft knife.

Pencil Sharpener

You'll need a pencil sharpener when using pencils of any kind. Some people simply use a craft knife to point a pencil. A small handheld sharpener is a great addition to a travel kit.

Metal Ruler

A ruler is necessary for measuring and drawing straight lines. A metal ruler is best for use with a craft knife because there is no risk of cutting into the ruler like there is with a wooden or plastic ruler.

Sponges

A big cleanup sponge is handy to have around, as are smaller ones for applying paint and certain image transfers. You could even use your kitchen sponge.

Large Tray

For a couple of the image transfer techniques we'll cover in Section Two, you'll need to soak your images in water. This can easily be done in a large tray. You can also use an old cake pan or casserole dish, a butcher's tray (found at fine arts stores) or a large plastic bucket.

FODDER

WORK SPACE

The ephemera of everyday life is at the heart of our journals. Employing ephemera is a great way to add memories into the journal, and as you collect your ephemera, you can begin thinking about how you will use the journal. You can easily store fodder in boxes and trays. Placing some of your material in a large plastic or manila envelope works well to make fodder portable. Try collecting some of the following:

One of the final things to think about as you start your journey is your work space. Where will you work? Having a private studio is great, but many people do not have that luxury. Find a space—a table, a desk or a corner—where you can leave out all of your supplies so they are always ready when you want to work. You do not want to spend most of your time setting up and cleaning up. With a space that is perpetually ready, you have the luxury of getting to work in your journal in a matter of minutes whenever you want.

- PHOTOS—YOUR OWN, THOSE OF OTHERS OR FROM MAGAZINES
- FLYERS
- POSTCARDS
- BROCHURES
- TICKETS—FROM MOVIES, PLAYS, SPORTING EVENTS, ETC.
- STICKERS
- SPECIALTY PAPERS—CONSTRUCTION, HANDMADE, VELLUM
- NEWSPAPER
- TELEPHONE BOOKS
- ENVELOPES
- MAPS
- COMPUTER PRINTOUTS
- PHOTOCOPIES
- BUSINESS CARDS
- GREETING CARDS
- LABELS
- WRAPPERS—FROM CANDY, GIFTS
- OLD ARTWORK
- LETTERS
- CALENDARS
- CARTOONS AND COMICS
- NAME TAGS
- FABRIC
- MENUS
- RECEIPTS
- NOTES
- PLAYING CARDS
- PUZZLE BOOKS
- OLD BOOKS
- LISTS
- STICKY NOTES
- PRESSED FLOWERS AND PLANTS

THE BASIC JOURNAL KIT

With all the choices to be made about
art supplies and equipment, the
visual journal can seem a daunting
undertaking, but getting started
is easy. A kit of commonly used and
inexpensive materials is a quick
way to begin the journey. All a
visual journalist needs to start
is a journal, a pair of scissors, a
glue stick and some favorite pens
and markers. Place these items in a
plastic bag, pencil case or artist
brush bag and you have portability.
As you gain experience with media and
concepts, you may want to add other
supplies to your journal kit; brushes,
watercolor paint and watercolor
pencils are common additions.
Beautiful and rich pages can be made
using these simple materials.

THE TRAVEL KIT

Being able to take a few
favorite materials along with
you as you go through your
day is invaluable for working
in your journal anywhere at
any time. An ideal travel kit
includes:
➤ a few pens, pencils and
markers
➤ a paintbrush, a small set of
watercolor pencils and/or paint
➤ scissors, a glue stick and
a plastic bag for collecting
fodder
The key here is to think small
so you remain mobile. You would
not want to have a large set of
colored pencils with you because
its bulk would end up slowing
you down.

JOURNAL PREP WORK

Now that you have your journal and some basic supplies, it's time to get the journal ready and to get yourself set up. Here are some of the rituals that we go through when starting a new journal. Of course, they are just possibilities, but we find these steps can often calm the anxiety of diving right in. If you want to skip these warm-ups and just get started, check out Section Two.

CoveR

Personalizing the cover of your journal can help you claim ownership and make it something special. Use durable acrylic paint. Glue pictures and photos on with acrylic gel medium and seal them with more gel medium. Collect stickers from various sources and plaster the cover like an old steamer trunk. Use opaque paint markers to draw and write on the cover. Some visual journalists create elaborate covers by cutting into and building onto existing covers. You are limited only by your imagination when it comes to personalizing the cover. Allow it to dry thoroughly before you use your journal. It is a good idea to seal the cover with gel medium or an acrylic varnish.

inside CoveR

The inside cover of your journal is a great place to put your identifying information. That way if you are separated from your journal and someone finds it, they can get in touch with you. Offering a reward also encourages the return of a lost or misplaced journal.

Other information can go on the inside cover as well. After reading Robert Kaupelis's *Experimental Drawing*, we adapted the oath he encourages his readers to write in the front of every sketchbook create what we call the visual journalist's oath: "I solemnly promise that from this day forward I shall never again be caught without a journal during my waking hours, and also that I shall use it faithfully every day."

Although the visual journal is always in a state of becoming, never truly finished, dates of initiation and retirement provide a way to keep track of the chronology of your visual journals. This may not seem like such a big deal if this is your first journal, but after you have ten or eleven filled visual journals sitting on a shelf, you may find it difficult to tell which one was first or second or fifth as the years blur together.

CalendaR

Who needs a day planner when you have a visual journal? If you have trouble keeping track of dates, putting a calendar in your journal is a great way to keep yourself organized. Think about drawing a calendar, gluing in a small one, or printing and gluing in monthly calendars from your computer. We find that having a separate planner or calendar does not work as well for us as having one in our journals because it is easy to neglect anything we don't have with us and use all the time.

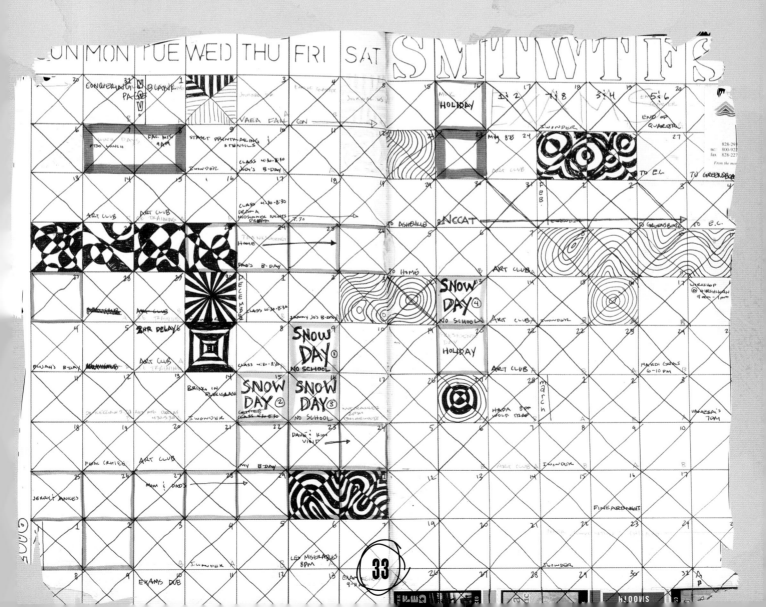

4. Independence

1. goals
reach up
for your
goals

3. GROWTH

2. RELATIONSHIP

5. STABILITY
No change

APPEARANCE

every PERCEIVABLE THING HAS FORM

EVER. MEANING HAS BEHAVIOR. CAN BE EITHER

CONCEPT
freedom
ocean
surfing
BEAUTY of

You do not
have
to be

Afraid of something that
is not part of
your world.

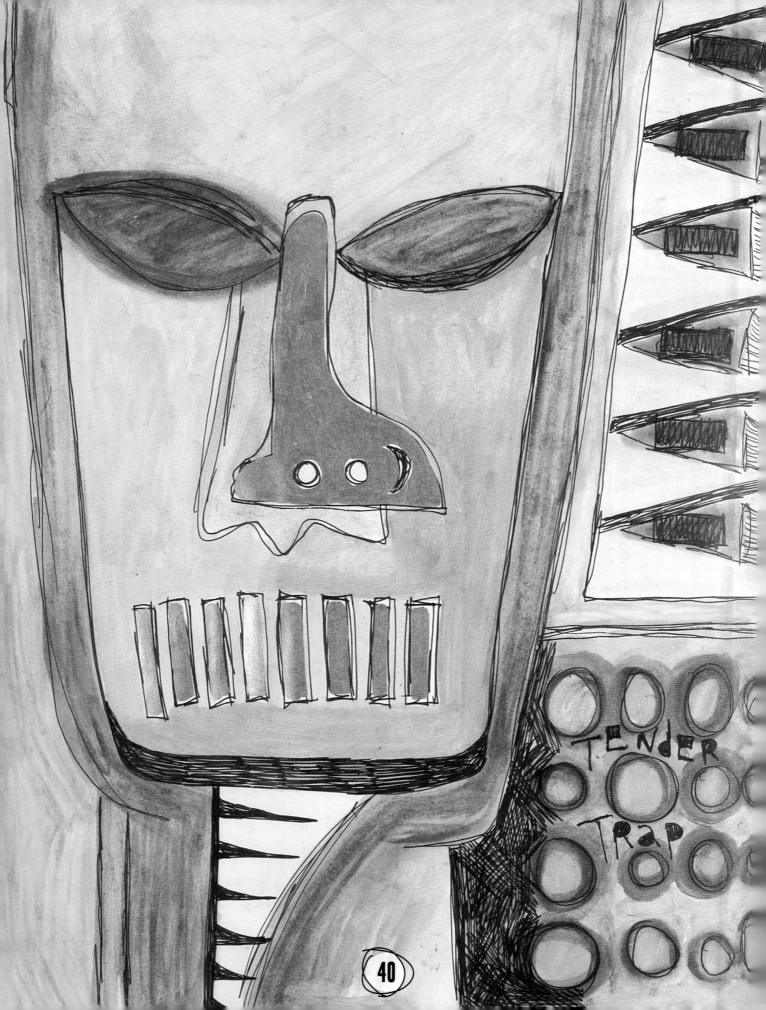

SECTION TWO
BASIC TRAINING

So you have a journal and some basic supplies, and you may have completed some of the rituals for preparing for your journey. Now you are ready to dive in. Opening a journal and facing blank pages can be overwhelming for any visual journalist. Fear of making mistakes or of not knowing what to do can stop even the most experienced. But push past your uncertainty and just get going with a page. A page that is no longer blank has an amazing way of quieting the inner critic.

The techniques and media discussed in the following pages are not about creating a particular image. They are about getting some color and shapes onto a page in order to start the journey. By getting a simple initial layer down, you can quell anxieties and encounter the blank page with confidence. You don't need to know exactly what a page will look like when it is finished. There are no mess-ups or mistakes if you can accept the accidental as part of the process. What some might see as a mess-up is only evidence of the journey on which your journal is focused. It's about the process, not the end product. Worrying about what your journal will look like when it's finished will only make you tighten up and block your creativity.

Free yourself from linear progression and begin the process. You may want to skip a few pages in your journal, or you may want to select a random page to start your journey. You can even use all the following techniques and media to begin something on every page. What's important is to enjoy the act and experiment freely. Try to remember the pure joy you experienced as a child creating art simply because you loved to create. Our own first journals seem sparse and underdeveloped compared to our most recent journals. Depth and meaning will slowly develop as you continue.

WATERCOLOR

Watercolor paint is a fast and effective way to add color, lines, shapes and textures to a page. Within a few minutes, you can get several pages under way. Entire books have been written and classes taught about watercolor, and it is not our intention to give you a comprehensive overview of the medium. We just want to impart some of the basic techniques that will allow you to explore and experiment with its unique and interesting effects.

WASH

You can quickly add color to a page by mixing a little bit of watercolor paint with water and spreading it over the paper with a large paintbrush. Remember that the color does not have to be even and smooth. Texture and variation in the paint add visual interest.

SUPPLIES
Paintbrush, water, watercolor paint

1 Dip a brush in water and swirl the wet brush into a chosen color of watercolor paint. Create a puddle of paint in the pan or palette. Brush the wet paint onto a page.

2 Vary the darkness of the wash. The longer you swirl your brush in the watercolor paint, the more pigment you get on the brush and the darker value you achieve, as in the upper left of this page. By dipping the brush in more water, you can lighten the value, as in the lower right of this page.

BLEEDING

When you allow two different colors of paint to bleed together, color mixing occurs. You can paint a page so that it gradually changes from one color to another, or you can add spots and lines of color that bleed into one another. The key is to work quickly and allow wet colors to touch each other as you work.

SUPPLIES
Paintbrush, water, watercolor paint

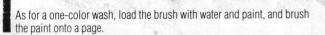

1 As for a one-color wash, load the brush with water and paint, and brush the paint onto a page.

2 Quickly rinse the brush to remove all of the first color and load the brush with a second. You do not want the paint on the page to dry, so work quickly.

3 Brush the second color onto the page, allowing it to touch, mix with and bleed into the first color.

Notice how the red gradually changes to the yellow-orange.

SPONGING

Sponge painting was a fad a few years ago in home decorating. You can use the same technique on a smaller scale in your journal.

SUPPLIES

Small sponge, water, watercolor paint, paintbrush

1 Dampen a small sponge by dipping it in water and squeezing out the excess.

2 Lightly dab the sponge into a selected color of paint. This can be a bit cumbersome if the sponge is large.

3 Alternatively you can brush the paint onto the sponge to cover a larger area.

4 Press the sponge onto the page to apply the paint. By manipulating the sponge in different ways, you can create regular or irregular patterns. Experiment. The finished page has a soft texture. You can sponge other colors onto the page as well.

STAMPING

Paint your hand, bubble wrap, plastic mesh, rubber stamps and fingers, and then press them onto a page before the paint dries. Explore stamping with a variety of objects and surfaces to discover your favorite textures.

SUPPLIES

Paintbrush, water, watercolor paint, object for stamping (bubble wrap)

1 Paint an object with a wash of watercolor (if using bubble wrap, make certain to paint the side with the bubbles). You can even apply multiple colors. Cover as much or as little of the object as desired.

2 Place the object on a page with the painted side down.

3 Lightly apply pressure to the back of the object and perhaps allow some drying time.

4 Lift the object to reveal the stamped texture or shape. You can rinse the object and reuse it later.

LIFTING

Lifting wet paint from the page lightens certain areas and creates value variations. Use a paper towel, a dry or slightly damp sponge, a cotton ball or a cotton swab to lighten darker areas. Use plastic wrap, aluminum foil, bubble wrap, plastic mesh or other objects to create textures and patterns.

SUPPLIES

```
Paintbrush, water, watercolor
paint, object for lifting
(plastic wrap)
```

1 Cover a page with a wash of watercolor paint.

2 Before the wash dries, place plastic wrap on the page. Allow the wrap to wrinkle and fold. The wet paint will gather and puddle under the plastic.

3 Allow the paint to dry and remove the plastic wrap to reveal a texture.

SALT

When you sprinkle ordinary table salt onto wet watercolor, the salt draws in water and paint, leaving a lightened area with a speckled texture behind. Small drops of rubbing alcohol can achieve a similar effect, but the marks are rounder, like the drops of alcohol.

SUPPLIES
Paintbrush, water, watercolor paint, salt

1 Paint a dark, wet wash of paint onto a page.

2 Lightly sprinkle ordinary table salt on the wet paint and allow the paint to dry completely.

3 Brush the salt off the page to reveal the texture. This technique does not work well on thinner, more absorbent paper.

STIPPLING

Stippling with watercolor is simple to do with a toothbrush by using your thumb or finger to flick the bristles after loading them with paint. This can be very messy, so be careful not to splatter the paint everywhere.

SUPPLIES

Toothbrush, water, watercolor paint

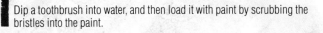

1 Dip a toothbrush into water, and then load it with paint by scrubbing the bristles into the paint.

2 Use a finger or your thumb to pull back the bristles and release them, producing a fine mist of paint. Pull your finger from the front of the toothbrush to the back.

3 Repeat until you have covered as much of the page as desired. Notice that sometimes when there is a lot of water in the toothbrush, large drops of color drip onto the page. Accidents like these are part of the process.

STENCILING

Plastic stencils and watercolor paint may not seem like such a great pairing because the wet paint has a tendency to run and bleed, but by using only a small amount of water, you can achieve effective results, and even the running and bleeding can prove beneficial. Wire and plastic mesh also work well as stencils if you're going for a gridlike texture.

SUPPLIES

Stencil, paintbrush, water, watercolor paint

1 Place a plastic stencil onto the page.

2 Load a brush with just a little water and some paint and lightly tap the brush into the stencil.

3 Try stenciling through plastic mesh to create texture.

4 Remove the stencil. The watercolor may bleed.

WATERCOLOR PENCIL

Watercolor pencil is a fast and easy way to lay down color for the initial layer of a page or to begin layering on top of dry watercolor. You can use the pencils like ordinary colored pencils, but the real fun begins when you introduce some water and water-based media. Experiment with techniques while trying to fill pages. By doing so, you can build a bank of started pages. You can use these same techniques with water-soluble graphite and water-soluble crayons.

·· ACTIVATE WITH WATER ··

Brushing water over watercolor pencil is probably the most common way to use this water-soluble media to achieve painterly effects. The opportunities are vast: You can create lines, shapes and words, or you can fill an entire page with color.

SUPPLIES
Watercolor pencil, paintbrush, water

1 Select a watercolor pencil and apply the color to the page. Press firmly and apply a lot of pigment. You can control the value by shading with the pencil and lightening up on the pressure.

2 Dip a paintbrush into clean water and brush over the places you applied watercolor pencil. The color will blend into the water.

3 You can make crisp lines and shapes by paying attention to the edges.

ACTIVATE WITH WATERCOLOR PAINT

Brush a layer of watercolor paint over watercolor pencil of a contrasting color to create a color blend. You will have to rinse out the brush before getting more watercolor paint so you do not contaminate the paint with the pigment from the pencil.

SUPPLIES

Watercolor pencil, paintbrush, water, watercolor paint

1 Select a watercolor pencil and apply the color to the page. Press firmly to get a lot of pigment on the page.

2 Dip a paintbrush into water, and then load your brush with watercolor paint of a contrasting color. Do not choose a color that will result in a muddy combination. Brush the paint onto the page, allowing it to mix and blend into the watercolor pencil.

3 Before getting more paint, thoroughly rinse your brush to avoid contaminating your watercolor. Load your brush with more watercolor and continue to paint.

ACTIVATE WITH MARKER

A water-based marker used over watercolor pencil adds up to a vibrant color blend. This technique leaves a lot of the watercolor pencil pigment on the marker tip, so you may want to have markers that you use only for this technique. Also, this technique is not effective with darker markers because the darker marker overpowers the watercolor pencil. All watercolor pencils will change in some way when blended with water-based marker. It can be interesting to overlap different colors or to purposely mix red with yellow to create orange or combine blue with yellow to get green and so on.

SUPPLIES
Watercolor pencil, waterbased marker

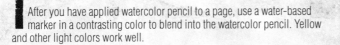

1 After you have applied watercolor pencil to a page, use a water-based marker in a contrasting color to blend into the watercolor pencil. Yellow and other light colors work well.

2 Continue until you have filled as much of the page as desired. The tip of the marker can quickly get covered with watercolor pencil pigment. You may need to wipe the excess pigment from the marker tip if the ink doesn't flow.

DIP INTO WATER

Wetting the tip of a watercolor pencil gives it a rich tone. Be careful not to sharpen the pencil until it has dried completely because the wet tip is very soft. Do not leave the pencil sitting in water because the pigment will dissolve.

SUPPLIES

Watercolor pencil, water, paintbrush

1 Choose a watercolor pencil and dip the tip into the water. Hold it there for a moment to allow the water to soften the point.

2 Draw with the pencil on a dry page. Repeatedly dip the pencil back into the water to keep the tip soft.

3 If desired, you can brush water over the resulting marks. Because the pigment is wet when applied, it soaks into the paper more and does not bleed very much.

DRAW INTO WET PAPER

You can work watercolor pencil into wet paper as well as dry. The look is similar to dipping the pencil into water, but more bleeding takes place. Be careful not to tear the wet page.

SUPPLIES
Paintbrush, water, watercolor paint (optional), watercolor pencil

1 Brush clean water or a wash of watercolor onto a page.

2 Working quickly, use the watercolor pencil to draw on the wet page. Be careful not to tear the paper.

3 You may need to apply more water if the page dries too quickly while you work.

ACTIVATE MULTIPLE COLORS

You can also achieve rich colors and textures by using multiple colors on a dry page before activating the watercolor pencil with water.

SUPPLIES
Watercolor pencil, water, paintbrush

1 Apply multiple colors of watercolor pencil to a dry page.

2 Beginning with the lighter colors, brush clean water onto the page.

3 Continue brushing water onto the page until you have covered as much of the page as desired.

WATERCOLOR PAINT & PENCIL

One of the things that sets our approach apart from that of some other visual journalists is the way we layer the work. By simply combining techniques and media, pages with a lot of depth emerge. The idea is to begin with one technique, let it dry if necessary, add another technique on top of the dry layer, let it dry if necessary, add another technique to create a third layer and so forth. You can have ten or fifteen layers on one page. You may want to set up a specific order for the techniques that you wish to layer.

Layering watercolor paint and watercolor pencil is an effective way to add visual interest to a page in its beginning stages. You can create a lot of different layers using these simple materials and techniques and can build up rich color variations and textures. You must allow each layer to dry completely to minimize bleeding. Then again, bleeding can be interesting. We'll add more to this page as we cover other materials and techniques in following sections.

1 Paint a wash of watercolor paint.

2 Stamp a darker color of watercolor with bubble wrap.

3 Stencil words, letters or numbers with watercolor.

4 Draw random lines with watercolor pencil and activate with clean water.

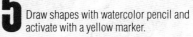

5 Draw shapes with watercolor pencil and activate with a yellow marker.

6 Dip a watercolor pencil into water and draw patterns all over the page.

In all my work there is some degree of content that is more obvious, communicating a specific or general idea that people will get. But a lot of times the content of the work is ambiguous enough that it can be interpreted by whoever. They aren't exactly telling you what they mean.

I see things in the street that are not intended to be art, but for me they're aesthetically interesting, so it's art to me. I see painted trucks or painted old, decaying billboards or something like that, to me, provide information and inspiration and some kind of visual, whatever. Something clicks in your head.

SOMETHING LIVED THROUGH KNOWLEDGE FROM LIFE

OT ALL WHO
WANDER
ARE LOST

151

PRIORITY MAIL
UNITED STATES POSTAL SERVICE ™
LABEL107R, OCT 1997   www.usps.gov

I crave life enriching and art enriching experiences.

Table MANNERS

1. SIT UP STRAIGHT
2. CHEW WITH YOUR MOUTH CLOSED
3. PUT YOUR NAPKIN IN YOUR LAP
4. SAY PLEASE & THANK YOU
5. TAKE SMALL BITES
6. DON'T PLAY WITH YOUR FOOD
7. HAVE PLEASANT CONVERSATION
8. KEEP YOUR ELBOWS OFF THE TABLE

Rich Ambiguity

How can we as artists activate the space of a work of art?

WELCOME ... YOU ARE ALMOST HOME

PARKING

		143	141	139	137	135	133	131	129	127	125			223		123
	249	247	245	243	241	239	237	235	233	231	229	227	225		221	121
250			244	242	240	238	236	234	232	230	228	226	224	*	219	119
150	148	146	144	142	140	138	136	134	132	130	128	126		120	217	117

FITNESS CENTER

153	253	252	152
157	255	254	154
159	257	256	156
161	259	258	158
163	261	260	160
165	263	262	162
167	265	264	164
169	269	268	168
171	271	270	170
173	273	272	172
175	275	274	174
177	277	276	176

PARKING

POOL

Holiday Inn EXPRESS

GREENSBORO NORTH CAROLINA

118		216	215	213	111
116		214	213		111
114		212	211		111
112		210			111
110		208	209	107
108		206	207	105
106		204	205	103
		202	203	101
		200	201	

PARKING

VENDING ICE ICE **VENDING**

CONVENTION CENTER
Opening Fall 1999

BREAKFAST BAR*
REGISTRATION*

STAY SMART℠

THURSDAY NOVEMBER ③ 2005

Creating a Visual Journal

12 PM – 1:50 PM

Come explore the possibilities of a Visual Journal. A visual journal is a personal record, a tool for self-exploration and reflection, and an art form for expression. In this mixed-media hands-on workshop participants will explore the creative possibilities of the visual journal. Various activities will be provided to experiment with media, techniques, and concepts. Bring a neglected or under-utilized sketchbook, scissors, glue stick, and any personal ephemera that will inspire your journal pages. Handouts, limited supplies and instruction will be provided.

Presenters:
Eric M. Scott
David R. Modler

ROOM Z

ORAGMI DOG

ON MY OWN

④ Independence

5. Stability

No Change

✝ 3. Relationships

Reaching

2. Goals

⑥ 1. GROWTH

Life Line to Art: Developing A Visual Diary

common thread to all forms of art

PRESENTERS
Nita Adams
Marce Miller
Lynne Mulhern

ROOM
17
3:10 PM–
4:00 PM

SOME OF THE BEST THINGS IN LIFE ARE FREE.

This presentation explores techniques used to record personal emotion, hue and media in a personal diary. These techniques will produce a magical journey from kindergarten to advance placement and will produce a body of visual notes and ideas that can be used for a formal body of work.

- **Model** art making
- Practice / Plan / Progress — **3P's**
- Provides exercises
- a tool for providing a way to view progress
- Create for yourself
- a way to transition
- Creates community
- Tool for learning and practice

habit ④ life

DOCUMENT
OBSERVE
IMAGINE

DRAW
WRITE
COLLAGE
COLLECT

ANALYSIS IN VERBAL REALM

WHAT ② do?
- journal a color you do not use
- what inspires your creativity
- what saps your creativity
- Oscar Blumner (Artist to check out)
- use art to express that **I AM**
- play on words
- journal a number
- journal a letter
- journal a word
- journal your safety zone
- sample each principle of design
- The Blank — Inviting the Muse — Anna Held Audette

RV CA

BARRY   McGEE

DRAWING REQUIRES COURAGE

COLLAGE

At the heart of a journal is its fodder, the ephemera from day-to-day life that we tend to collect and cherish. We often relegate these precious bits to boxes, drawers and envelopes. There our mementoes remain hidden and safe until we stumble across them, perhaps years later. The visual journal is a perfect place to save these wonderful items, and fodder is a perfect way to make meaning from personal images.

Fodder is not necessarily the precious mementoes we have kept for a lifetime. It can be the mundane material of our lives: scraps of paper, envelopes, random doodles, receipts and whatever else may be lying around. When you select these materials and place them in the journal, you transform them. They become a record of where you are and what you've been doing. Plain and simple things take on greater significance when they become visual cues for memory, helping to tell the story of our lives in more comprehensive ways. For example, you can write about having gone to see a movie, but by gluing in the ticket stub, you can merge image with text and tell a more complete narrative. By gluing in pieces of fodder, you can plant the seeds of a wonderful page.

Explore your fodder and pick a piece that feels right. Find the right spot for it in your journal by trusting your gut reaction. We have innate sensibilities that we often ignore in our quest to get it right.

You want to be careful when you glue in collage elements. Often too little glue results in the piece falling out of the journal, or too much glue accidentally adheres pages together. You also need to be mindful of the texture of the fodder. You may run into difficulties with slick, uneven, thick or rough surfaces. For these surfaces, you may need to use extra glue, or you may have to switch to a heavy-duty glue like book-binding paste.

Often it is not the kind of glue but the way an item is glued that keeps the collage elements adhered to the page. The following procedure is a good guideline for getting fodder to stick in the journal.

GLUING FODDER INTO THE JOURNAL

A glue stick is probably the most versatile adhesive and the most appropriate for many things, from copy paper to cardstock.

SUPPLIES

Fodder, scissors, glue stick, scrap paper, burnisher (optional)

1 Trim the piece of fodder if necessary.

2 Turn the piece of fodder over onto a piece of scrap paper. Press firmly with the glue stick and cover the entire back of the collage piece with glue.

3 Place the fodder on the page.

4 Gently rub the fodder with your hands or a burnisher. Consider placing a piece of scrap paper over the collage element as you rub in case any excess glue oozes out.

PAGE ALTERING

As you work in the journal, you are not limited to experimenting with art materials and gluing in fodder. You are free to experiment with the page itself. You can physically alter pages to produce visual effects and to bring some interactivity to your journal. Certain techniques lend themselves to making the journal more interactive by giving the viewer glimpses and peeks into other pages as well as by allowing the viewer to open envelopes and pockets, and to reveal hidden spaces behind doors and folds.

FOLDING

The simplest way to alter a page is to fold it. A simple fold creates instant interactivity because every reader wants to see what is behind the fold. Folds are good for hiding things, making areas of surprise and creating instant doors. Folds bring another visual level to the journal by allowing pages to interact with one another, creating visual links between them.

1 Select two blank pages.

2 Fold both pages into the center of the book. Unfold the pages and you are ready to create.

The following images show only some of the many different page interactions you can achieve with two simple folds.

Both pages folded.

Both pages unfolded.

Both folded pages to the left.

The left folded page completely opened.

The right folded page completely opened.

The left folded page opened in the opposite direction.

DOORS

You can cut a door into a page so that it reveals something on another page. A door adds instant interactivity just like a fold because viewers will want to open it and look. You can make a door simply by folding a page or by gluing a blank card to a page. You can make a door even more quickly from a single piece of paper using a craft knife. Experiment with the different ways in your journal.

SUPPLIES
Pencil, cutting mat, craft knife

1 Draw a line as a guide for cutting.

2 Place a cutting mat under the page, and use a craft knife to cut through. In this case, we cut both pages to create a circle around the brain image.

TIP

When using a craft knife, you need to use a sharp blade and a lot of caution. A sharp blade cuts more easily and cleanly than a dull blade. Be extremely careful not to cut yourself or the underlying pages.

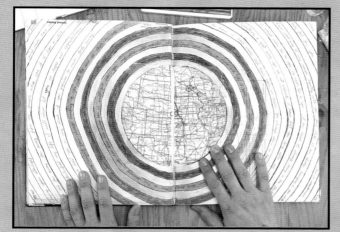

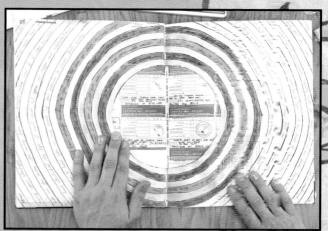

The cut area open in one direction to reveal a portion of a map.

The cut portion open in the opposite direction to reveal labels.

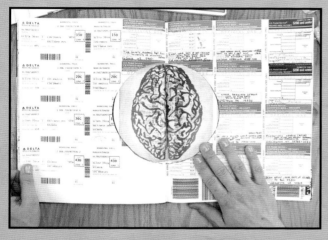

The outer portion flipped in one direction to reveal the brain on the label page.

The cut portion flipped to reveal the map on the label page.

The outer portion flipped the opposite direction to reveal the brain on the map page.

WINDOWS

Windows and holes in pages give glimpses into other pages and create relationships between them. Using a craft knife and cutting mat, you can quickly cut holes and windows in pages without cutting into their neighbors.

SUPPLIES

Cutting mat, craft knife, glue (optional)

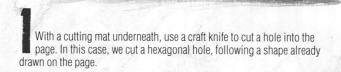

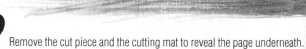

1 With a cutting mat underneath, use a craft knife to cut a hole into the page. In this case, we cut a hexagonal hole, following a shape already drawn on the page.

2 Remove the cut piece and the cutting mat to reveal the page underneath.

3 You can turn the page to expose the cut out section on two different pages and choose how to embellish the areas. Here we turned the page to show a blank area.

In this case, we embellished the space on the previous page and glued the cut piece elsewhere.

SINGEING

Burning the edges of pages or even areas within pages with a candle or lighter is another way to alter your journal. Large burnt holes and edges can give glimpses into other pages. Always be careful when using flames. You do not want to set your journal or work space on fire!

SUPPLIES
Lighter

1 Singe the edge of a page. You may want to tilt the page if you want the flames to burn in a particular direction.

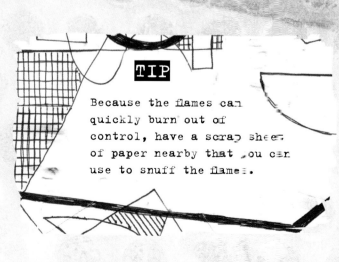

2 Singe a hole into a page. Hold the page up if you do not want to burn the underlying pages.

3 Allow the flame to burn through several pages to create pages that interact with one another.

TIP

Because the flames can quickly burn out of control, have a scrap sheet of paper nearby that you can use to snuff the flames.

TEARING

Tearing the edges of pages creates the opportunity for interactions between them. A series of torn pages can be visually and psychologically interesting. The difference between the smooth edge of the manufactured page and the jagged, torn edge infuses tension. This particular tearing technique yields the look of four successive torn pages while tearing only two.

SUPPLIES

Scoring tool, cutting mat, ruler, glue

1 Choose two pages to tear. (These pages have been painted orange and yellow to make the process more visible.) Tear the top page (in this case, the orange one) down the middle.

2 Tear the second page (in this case, the yellow one). You can control the tear to make it more interesting by going slowly.

3 Score both torn pieces about ½" (1cm) to 1" (3cm) from what used to be the edges.

4 Use a bone folder to fold over both edges, creating tabs for gluing.

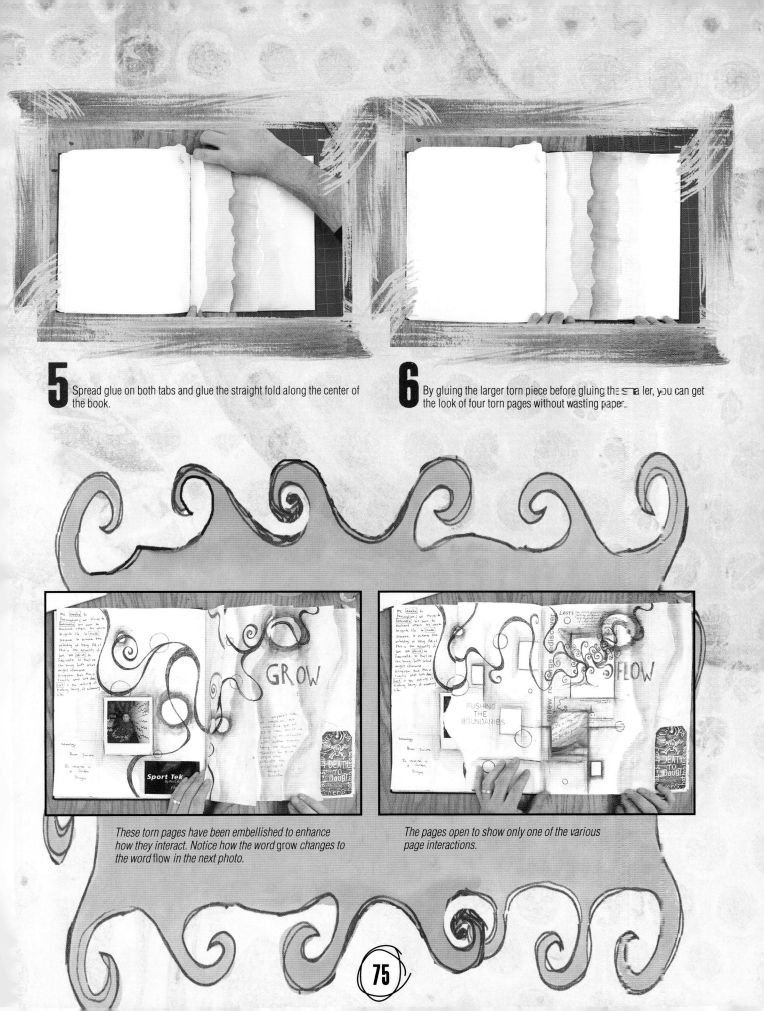

5 Spread glue on both tabs and glue the straight fold along the center of the book.

6 By gluing the larger torn piece before gluing the smaller, you can get the look of four torn pages without wasting paper.

These torn pages have been embellished to enhance how they interact. Notice how the word grow *changes to the word* flow *in the next photo.*

The pages open to show only one of the various page interactions.

POCKETS

We tend to store loose fodder and papers randomly in our journals to use later. Unfortunately these items sometimes slip out and get lost. Putting pockets in your journal is invaluable for storing the fodder and ephemera that you collect and plan to use at a later time. You can also use pockets to create interaction in your journal as places to hold surprises, notes and small works of art. Think about how many pockets you want or need and where the pockets should go. You can glue in a large envelope for a pocket, make one from additional paper and some tape, or cut a page in half and seal the edges with tape.

SUPPLIES
Glue, ruler, pen, scissors, tape

1 Spread glue over an entire page and glue the next page to it. This thickens the paper, making for a sturdier pocket.

2 Use a ruler to draw a horizontal line near the center of the thickened page. Measure if you want.

3 Cut along the horizontal line to create two flaps.

4 Glue the top flap to the previous page.

5 Use the bottom flap to create the pocket by taping its side and bottom. We used packaging tape here, but you could use duct tape, masking tape or even bumper stickers.

6 Flip over the page and pocket and fold the tape around the edge to the other side.

7 Smooth out the tape, and rub or burnish to make a tight seal.

8 Check the strength and integrity of the pocket before using it.

A manila envelope creates a pocket for small works of art.

A decorative envelope also makes an effective pocket.

POP-UPS

Pop-ups are naturally surprising and fun. Here we show you how to make simple pop-ups with folded paper. More complex pop-ups are beyond the scope of this book, but there are many wonderful resources that can help you learn more.

SUPPLIES

Loose paper, scoring tool, ruler, glue

1 Fold a piece of paper in half and score a straight line at the two opposing edges parallel to the fold to create tabs for gluing.

2 Fold the tabs on the scored lines.

SPECIAL FORCES TRAINING

Take a look at Elements of Pop-Up: A Pop-Up Book for Aspiring Paper Engineers, by David A. Carter and James Diaz, for more ideas and how-tos for creating pop-ups.

3 Unfold the tabs and apply glue to the outside of them. Place the folded paper into the journal near its center.

4 Close the previous page on top of the pop-up.

5 Rub the page to make certain the tabs stick to both pages.

6 Open the page to reveal the pop-up ready for embellishment.

DRAWING

Many people want to run away screaming when they hear the word *drawing* because they believe they are not artists or that they have no talent for it. People run into trouble when they start thinking that only highly detailed, ultrarealistic renderings constitute good drawing. But the joy that we understood as children of just making marks is what we are after here—not a high-stress, "it's got to be perfect" mind-set. The fact is that drawing is like any artistic technique—anyone can learn to do it, and the more you do it, the better you get at it. If drawing still stresses you out, try simpler low-risk techniques. Keep in mind that you do not always need to draw with a pen or a pencil. Use any and all drawing media and experiment with a variety of materials to explore each one's characteristics.

LINES AND SHAPES

Without overthinking it, draw random lines and shapes on a page. Divide the page into several large areas by drawing several lines so they cross the page in every direction, or fill a page with a variety of one shape or multiple shapes. Take your pencil for a walk by allowing your hand to slowly meander across the page, letting the lines overlap. Whether you draw lines and shapes freehand or with a tool, turn off the inner critic that calls for you to do it perfectly. Find joy in simply making marks!

SUPPLIES
Pen, marker or pencil

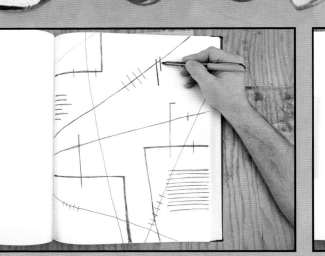

Straight lines: Try your hand at horizontal, vertical, diagonal, parallel and perpendicular. Mix them up!

Squares and rectangles: Vary the size. Overlap shapes and change directions.

Circles: Vary the size and think about overlapping.

A variety of lines and shapes: Play with size and line thickness. Allow some lines to go off the edge of the page.

Triangles: Experiment with type and direction. Consider isosceles, acute, obtuse and equilateral triangles.

Jagged or zigzag lines: Create patterns or juxtapose them for contrast. Play with line thickness.

Curved lines: Draw them from top to bottom or side to side. Have them run off the edges or stop when they intersect.

Curling, irregular lines: As you draw these lines, ideas about maps and pathways can emerge.

TRACING

Some people think tracing is cheating, but we think that's silly. Remember, your purpose is to get a shape, a letter or an image onto the paper, so anything that helps is fine to use. Hold the object you are tracing firmly so it does not shift. Be mindful that you may leave marks on your object or stencil—don't use any object you don't want ruined.

SUPPLIES

Pen, object to trace

Trace circular objects like bottles and jars.

Trace your hand and others' hands.

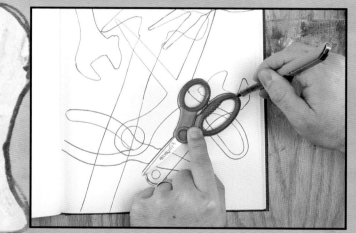
Trace tools and equipment like scissors and pliers.

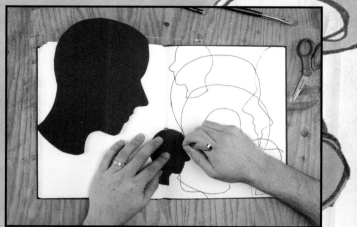
Trace cutouts like these profiles cut from cardstock.

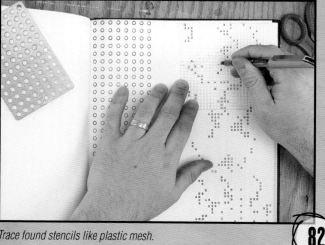
Trace found stencils like plastic mesh.

Trace letter, number and shape stencils.

DOODLING

How often have you found yourself doodling while talking on the phone, sitting in a meeting or waiting for someone? Doodling is a great way to add spontaneity to your journal. It's also a unique way to keep a record of your subconscious thoughts. The images and words that emerge while doodling can spark more complex ideas and pages.

SUPPLIES
Pen

Let your mind wander and don't overthink it. See what your imagination comes up with.

ANALOG DRAWING

An analog drawing depicts an emotion using a variety of lines, shapes, values and colors. Simply quiet your mind for a moment (close your eyes if you like), and then attempt to feel the emotion that you want to express. Allow the feeling to well up inside of you; feel it within your body; visualize it. Now draw what that feeling looks like. The idea is to channel the emotion right out of your hand, through your drawing tool and onto the paper.

SUPPLIES
Pen

This analog drawing depicts the feeling of joy. The spiraling lines burst out from the center giving a sense of excitement. The short lines and dots look like confetti.

OBSERVATIONAL DRAWING

Just try looking at an object and drawing what you see. Anxiety comes from telling ourselves that we cannot draw and that our drawings need to be perfect and realistic. You may find that you are better at drawing than you thought. In any case, with a little practice you can vastly improve.

This photo shows my hand right next to the drawing I'm working on only to give you an idea of what's going on. In reality you wouldn't want the object you're drawing so near the drawing. You're not supposed to see your work as you do it.

blind contour drawing

Blind contour drawings involve looking very closely at an object and drawing without looking at your drawing. Your eyes stay trained on the object, looking very carefully at its edges (or contours)—both the outer edges of the object and the edges of features and elements within the object.

Place your journal on a table. Turn your chair away from the table so you can put your drawing hand in a comfortable position, slightly behind you, and hold an object in your other hand or look at something within your field of vision. Observe the object carefully for a few moments. Pick a spot where it makes sense to begin and place your pencil or pen on the paper. Start to trace the edges of the object with your eyes very slowly. Allow your pencil to follow along, recording the movement of your eyes along the object. The key is to go very slowly—eyes and hand moving in coordination—while not looking at the drawing. You are training your eyes to observe very closely and your hand to record those observations. Keep going until you have traced all the outer contours of the object and the edges within the object. If you find that your pen or pencil goes off the page, simply place it back on without looking at the page.

After you finish, look at the drawing. If you have gone slowly and not looked, your drawing should not look like the object you were drawing. Because you did not look at the drawing, you had no way to judge size and proportion. That is the way these drawings are supposed to look. Some people are horrified at the results because the drawing doesn't look like the object. Yet these can be wonderful and beautiful drawings when you accept the process. The purpose of this type of drawing is to improve your observational drawing skills. Try making several drawings on one page, perhaps turning the book every time you begin with a new object. The overlapping lines make a great basis for a page. The best part: There is no way to mess up.

continuous contour drawing

To make a continuous contour drawing, begin by sitting so you can see your journal page and the object you wish to draw. Look carefully at the object for a few minutes and observe its outer and inner edges. Pick a spot to begin and place your pen or pencil on the page. As you would for a blind contour drawing, allow your eyes to follow the contours of the object slowly and your pencil or pen to follow along on the paper. This time, you can look at the paper. However, do not pick up the pen or pencil. If you do pick up your pen or pencil, put it back down where you left off. You will have to make judgments as you go about length, size and proportion. As the drawing progresses, you will probably find you need to backtrack along lines already drawn or create a bridge to get to a feature within the object.

Continue until you have drawn all the contours of the object and its interior lines. Your drawing should look more like the object than a blind contour drawing, but don't expect an exact rendering. Because you kept your pen or pencil to the paper and could not erase, the drawing should be a little off. Again, accepting the process instead of rejecting an end result allows you to see the beauty of these drawings. As with the blind contour, drawing a continuous contour helps you train your eyes to really observe an object and your hand to record those observations.

modified contour drawings

Modified contour drawings allow you to look at the paper, pick up your pen or pencil and fix your mistakes. However, try not to get caught up in making your work perfect. Draw what you truly see and not what you think you should see. You are only trying to capture the contours of an object. Don't worry about shading. With a little practice, you can become quite proficient at these drawings and quickly record observations visually.

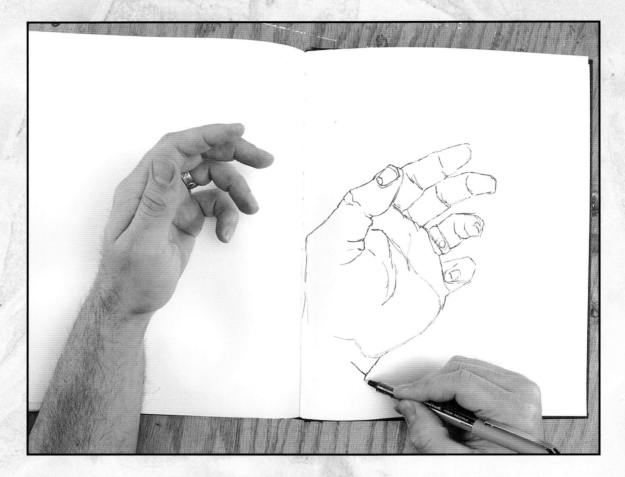

SPECIAL FORCES TRAINING

If you are interested in other drawing exercises, many resources are available. We highly recommend two books: Betty Edwards's Drawing on the Right Side of the Brain and Robert Kaupelis's Experimental Drawing.

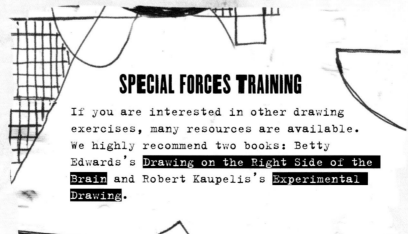

COLLAGE, PAGE ALTERING AND DRAWING

You can layer all the techniques you've learned—collage, page altering and drawing—onto pages to start piecing together meaning and themes. Let's go back to the layered example page that we started in the last section and add to it. (For the first six steps of this demonstration, see pages 56–57.)

7 Cut out some colored paper shapes and magazine images. Glue them onto the page.

8 Use a craft knife and cutting mat to cut holes into the page.

9 Use ink to draw and trace various shapes, words and letters on the page.

PHOTO RECONNAISSANCE

ardent

energy

considered a rejection of your artistic work. We do encourage you

among those sele

was not among those sele

We regret that your application was not among those sele

to apply again in the future. We are sorry.

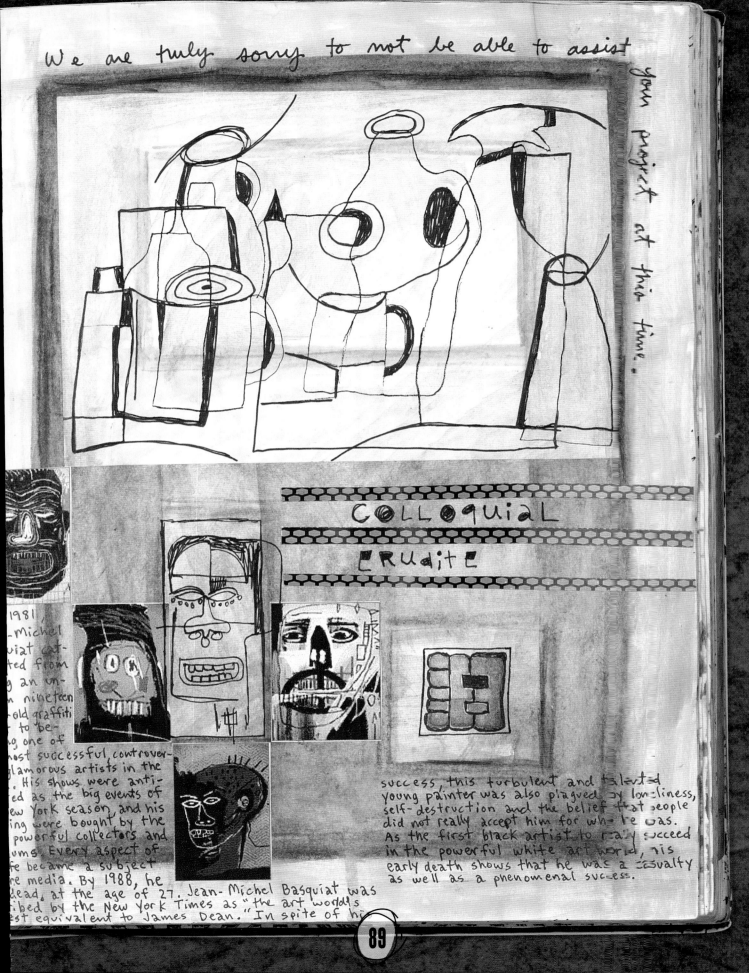

COLLOQUIAL

ERUDITE

1981, -Michel uiat cat- ted from g an un- n nineteen old graffiti r to be- g one of ost successful controver- lamorous artists in the . His shows were anti- d as the big events of w York season, and his ng were bought by the powerful collectors and ums. Every aspect of e became a subject re media. By 1988, he dead, at the age of 27. Jean-Michel Basquiat was ibed by the New York Times as "the art world's st equivalent to James Dean." In spite of hi

success, this turbulent and talented young painter was also plagued by loneliness, self-destruction and the belief that people did not really accept him for who he was. As the first black artist to really succeed in the powerful white art world, his early death shows that he was a casualty as well as a phenomenal success.

IF YOU AREN'T GOING ALL THE WAY WHY GO AT ALL?

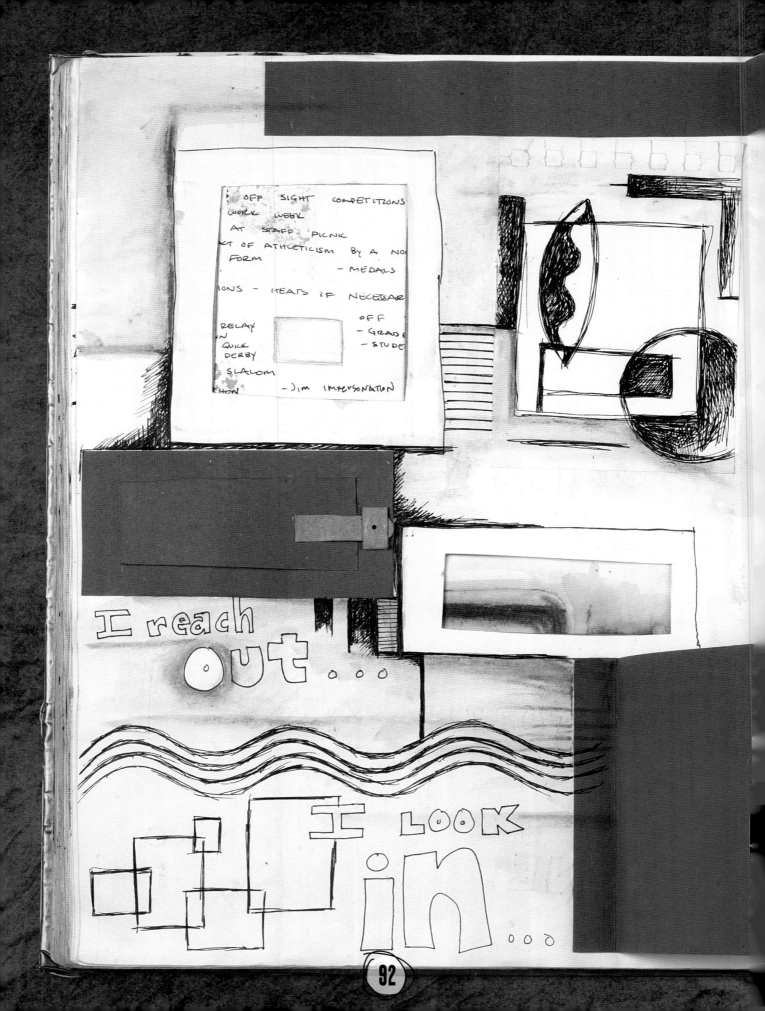

OFF SIGHT COMPETITIONS
WORK WEEK
AT STAFF PICNIC
...CT OF ATHLETICISM BY A NO...
FORM
                    - MEDALS

...IONS - HEATS IF NECESSAR...

RELAY   OFF
...IN   - GRADE...
QUICK   - STUDE...
DERBY

SLALOM

...HOW   - JIM IMPERSONATION

I reach
out ...

I LOOK
in
ooo

"DAVE WITH THE OFFICIAL FABLLE BAG"

MEN'S
S M L XL

REI
www.rei.com

REI
TRADITION
CYCLING

TESTED. TRUSTED.
GUARANTEED.

I have control over my minute universe. The smaller, the more control I have. When it becomes larger, I give up that control.

Outer Banks, N.C.

THE PAINTING HAS A
LIFE OF ITS OWN. I TRY
TO LET IT COME THROUGH.

JACKSON POLLOCK

IMAGE TRANSFERS

Image transfer techniques enable you to transfer an image from a source to a new surface and are ideally suited for use in mixed-media applications like the visual journal. Often solid collage images just do not work for a given situation, but a transparent or slightly distorted version of an image does work. Image transfers are ideal for adding imagery to a page when crisp, clean images aren't ideal.

Some techniques are suitable for layering pieces on top of existing imagery, and other techniques are more suitable for beginning with a fresh page and working other media into it. Some techniques are simple and direct; others are complicated and time-consuming. None of them give perfect results. As with any artistic technique, transfers have their limits. If you want perfect results, simply glue in the image as a collage element.

Basic materials and directions for five different image transfer techniques follow. Each technique comes with warnings and cautions. Be advised that there are risks with each and that each requires some practice. Also each technique works best with particular types of images. Experimenting with these image transfer techniques directly in your journal is a great way to master them.

Caution: Iron-on transfers involve the use of a hot iron. Use caution to avoid burning yourself, the transfer paper or surface. Every manufacturer has different recommendations for their papers, so follow all instructions and cautions as provided. Some distortion and bubbling may occur.

IRON-ON TRANSFERS

For iron-on transfers, you must use special paper that runs through an ink-jet printer. Normally these transfers are used on fabric, but you can also iron them onto a paper support.

SUPPLIES

Computer, ink-jet printer, iron-on transfer paper for ink-jet printers (found in most office supply stores), digital image, scissors, household iron

1 Print an image onto the iron-on transfer paper. Follow the directions that come with the paper. You may need to reverse the image so it is oriented correctly when transferred. Place the transfer with the image side down onto a page.

2
Following the manufacturer's directions, iron the back of the transfer paper. Be aware that crayon or tape could melt under the iron's heat.

3
Carefully peel back one corner of the backing paper to see how well the image has transferred. You may need to re-iron some sections that did not transfer.

4
Peel the paper completely off the transfer and allow it to cool.

5
You can use a variety of media to draw and write on top of the transfer. Here we're using a paint marker.

SOLVENT TRANSFERS

You can use solvents like xylene and acetone to transfer toner-based images—that is, photocopies, laser prints and magazine images. The technique will not work with ink-jet images, and the all-in-one scanners, printers and copiers that many of us have at home are usually just glorified ink-jet printers. Of the two chemicals, xylene seems to work the best for us.

SUPPLIES

Xylene or acetone product (Goof Off, Oops), cloth or sponge, photocopied laser-printed or magazine image, burnisher (nonplastic), glass container, blotter paper or newspaper

Caution: Xylene and acetone are very flammable and evaporate quickly. They must be used in a well-ventilated area because the fumes can be harmful and toxic. Read all labels and warnings before using either. Xylene will melt plastic, so do not store it in a plastic container.

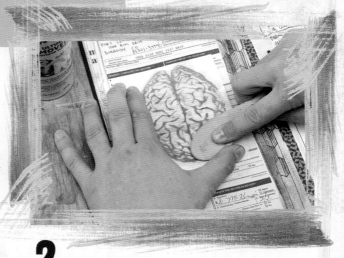

1 Place your image facedown on a page and moisten a cloth or sponge with the xylene. Rub the back of the image thoroughly with the cloth so the paper is saturated with the solvent.

2 Burnish the back of the image with a wooden spoon, bone folder or other nonplastic burnisher. Xylene will melt plastic.

TIP

These solvents can soak through multiple pages. Place blotter paper or newspaper under you page to prevent the chemical from affecting materials and images on other pages.

3 Carefully lift a corner of the image to see how it has transferred. You may need to apply more chemical or burnish harder if it has not transferred well. Lift off the image to reveal the transfer.

SOLVENT **MARKER** TRANSFERS

Some solvent markers contain xylene and are effective for transferring small images. They are a convenient alternative to using big bottles or jars of solvent—a great option for your travel kit.

SUPPLIES
Toner-based image, solvent marker

1 Place your image facedown onto a chosen page and apply the marker to the back of the image. It will moisten the paper with chemical, causing it to become translucent.

2 Often burnishing is not necessary because the marker burnishes as you apply the chemical. Lift one corner to check the transfer. Burnish with a wooden spoon or bone folder if necessary.

3 Remove the image to reveal the transfer.

TIP

Because magazine images have images on both sides, special caution is necessary. When using magazine photos, soak the receiver paper first with the chemical before placing the image, and place a piece of scrap paper on the back of the magazine image before burnishing. This will keep the mess to a minimum.

PACKAGING TAPE TRANSFERS

You can use ordinary clear packaging tape to quickly transfer newspaper, magazine, photocopied and black-and-white laser-printed images. This technique works to some degree with color laser-printed images as well.

SUPPLIES

Clear packaging tape, image, scissors, burnisher, bowl or small tub of water, sponge (optional), glue stick or acrylic medium

1 Cut the selected image to the desired size. Cutting straight edges allows for more control. Leave a little space around the image to be trimmed more closely later. Here we are transferring an image of Martin Luther King Jr. The image of Lincoln is on the back of the MLK image and will not be transferred.

2 Pull out some tape. With the sticky side up, lay the tape flat on the work surface. Static electricity holds it in place. Place the image you wish to transfer facedown onto the sticky side of the tape. You can see in this photo the image on the back. It will be rubbed away in the end. We have found this method of applying tape works best. Alternatively, attempting to place the tape onto the image causes wrinkles.

Caution: Some magazines work better than others, so experiment. Sometimes a fine film of paper will remain after the transfer no matter how long you rub. Sometimes the image will become scratched. (That may be a desirable effect.) This technique does not work with ink-jet prints. Because ink-jet ink is water soluble, it gets washed off the tape.

3 Cover the entire image using multiple strips of tape. Pick up the image after each strip is added and line up the next strip of tape. Overlap the strips slightly so the whole transfer stays intact.

4 After the entire image is covered, trim it down until only the parts you wish to transfer remain. You could even cut curved edges. This removes the excess tape and keeps your transfer from sticking to things as you work.

5 Rub the back of the transfer with a burnisher to ensure the image is thoroughly stuck to the tape. Rubbing the back of the image keeps the front of the transfer from scratching. Get out as many air bubbles as you can.

6 Soak the image in water for a few minutes. Warm water works well, but cold water is fine if you soak it longer.

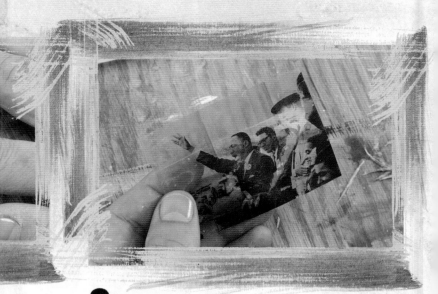

7 Remove the image from the water and place it tape side down on your work surface. Gently rub the back of the image with your finger to begin removing the paper. Put the image back in the water to soak longer if needed.

8 Continue to rub gently to remove all the paper. Sometimes a sponge works well for this. The image should be completely transparent with no paper pulp left. With some magazines, it may be difficult to remove all the paper, and the image will look frosted.

9 Allow the transfer to dry. Spread glue on the back. Although the tape may still be sticky, using a glue stick ensures that the transfer adheres well.

10 Press the transfer onto a journal page and rub with your hand or a burnisher to thoroughly adhere. Notice how you can see through the image.

ACRYLIC MEDIUM TRANSFERS

Acrylic medium transfers are very similar to packaging tape transfers except they take longer to do. This technique works with any acrylic medium, gloss, matte or gel. We like to use gel medium because it is thicker and requires fewer coats. We primarily use this with magazine images, but it works to some degree with laser prints and photocopies as well.

SUPPLIES

Acrylic medium (gloss, matte or gel), paintbrush, magazine image, scissors, scrap cardboard, craft knife, bowl or tub of water, sponge (optional)

1 Cut a magazine image to size and place it onto scrap cardboard with the image facing up. Brush the image in one direction with a thick layer of acrylic medium. The medium will look cloudy or milky. Wash the brush and allow the medium to dry completely. The medium should be clear when it is dry. Drying time varies with the thickness of the coat.

2 Paint another layer of medium in the opposite direction and allow it to dry. Wash the brush. Repeat until you've applied between five and ten layers. You're aiming for a thick skin on the image that will not tear.

Caution: Some magazines work better than others, so experiment. Sometimes a fine film of paper will remain no matter how long you rub. Sometimes the image gets scratched. If you store multiple acrylic medium transfers together, they may stick to each other.

3 The image will stick to the cardboard. Use a craft knife to remove the image from the cardboard by cutting around the edges.

4 Soak the image in water for a few minutes. Warm water works well, but cold water is fine if you soak it longer.

5 Remove the image from the water and place it on your work surface with the back of the image facing up. Gently rub the image with your finger to remove the paper. Soak again if needed. Continue to rub gently to remove all the paper. Sometimes a sponge works well for this.

6 Allow the image to dry completely. It should be fairly transparent.

7 Use acrylic medium to glue the transfer to the desired page by coating the back.

8 Place the image in the journal and rub with your hand or a burnisher to thoroughly adhere.

9 You can also brush a layer of medium over the transfer to make certain it is sealed onto the page. Allow it to dry thoroughly before closing the journal.

TIP

This is a very involved process to do for just one image. We usually make between five and ten acrylic medium transfers at a time.

INK-JET ACETATE TRANSFERS

Many transfer techniques do not work with ink-jet printers because of their water-soluble ink. Using a regular piece of acetate, also known as transparency film, makes it possible.

SUPPLIES
paper towels, computer and ink-jet printer, acetate (overhead transparencies are inexpensive), sponge, water, burnisher (optional)

1 Use a damp paper towel, rag or sponge to moisten a journal page. Do not soak the page. You want it to be only slightly damp.

2 Print an image onto the acetate using a regular ink-jet printer. You may want to reverse the image, especially if it contains text. The ink will be wet, so be careful not to touch or smudge the image. Place the acetate, ink side down, onto the damp page.

3 Use your hand or a burnisher to rub the back of the transfer.

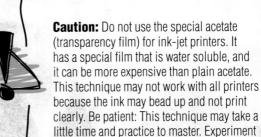

Caution: Do not use the special acetate (transparency film) for ink-jet printers. It has a special film that is water soluble, and it can be more expensive than plain acetate. This technique may not work with all printers because the ink may bead up and not print clearly. Be patient: This technique may take a little time and practice to master. Experiment to find what works best for you.

4 Lift a portion of the image to check how well it has transferred. Burnish areas if necessary.

5 Lift the acetate completely off the transfer.

6 Clean the acetate with a damp paper towel, rag or sponge. You can use the film again.

7 Allow the transfer to dry completely. Once dry, you can draw into it with a pen, marker or pencil.

ACRYLIC PAINT

Acrylic paint is ideal for mixed-media work, and the journal is no exception. Acrylic is suitable for any stage of a page, but it often works best as one of the last layers because it can be difficult to work on top of it.

There are some setup and cleanup concerns with acrylic paint because it is a polymer and turns into plastic when it dries. It is important not to allow the paint to dry in the paintbrush bristles because it can ruin them. Simply clean brushes with soap and water to maintain them. Many watercolor techniques work well with acrylic paint. Try sponging, stippling and stenciling.

OPACITY

Acrylic paint is extremely versatile. You can thin it with water and use it much like watercolor paint. You can change the value and opacity of the paint by varying the amount of water you add. We added more and more water to the blue paint in the photo below to create lighter and lighter values. Starting in the upper right corner of the palette and moving counterclockwise, the puddles of paint correspond to the painted samples in order from left to right.

MIX AND BLEND

It is perfectly acceptable to use acrylic paint straight from the tube or bottle, but by mixing and blending two or more paint colors, you can come up with seemingly endless color variations. Work quickly in small sections so the paint does not dry.

SUPPLIES
Paintbrush, acrylic paint, palette

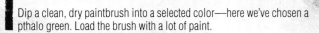

1 Dip a clean, dry paintbrush into a selected color—here we've chosen a pthalo green. Load the brush with a lot of paint.

2 Brush the color into a small area on a page. Work quickly so the paint doesn't dry.

3 Dip the brush into a contrasting color—in this case yellow. Do not clean out or rinse the brush. Allow the color that is already on the brush to mix with the new color.

4 Scoop out some of the contrasting paint and mix in a clean spot on the palette to create the new color—in this case yellow-green. Keep both original colors so you can continue the mixing and blending process all over the page. A little of the green is left in the yellow but not enough to affect further mixing.

5 Brush the new color next to the still wet color. Try not to allow the colors to touch.

6 After you've painted a small section, use the paintbrush to blend the colors together. You do not need to clean the brush. Using a short *X* motion between the colors works well to blend them. Try not to use large strokes and overblend because you will lose your original colors. Notice how the dark green gradually changes to yellow-green in our example.

7 Continue the process to fill as much of the page as desired. You may need to rinse and dry the brush before beginning again with the original color. You can even mix in a third color as you go to create more color variations. In this case, we've added white into the greens.

TEXTURING WITH SAND

When people explore our journals, they often like to feel the surface of the pages for the variety of textural effects. Many of these effects are made by the layering of images and collage elements, but you can fashion different textures by mixing other materials with the acrylic paint. Because the acrylic paint seals things onto the surface when dry, you can add almost anything to the paint to create textures on the page. To concoct quick textures with acrylic paint, try mixing in materials such as sand and salt.

SUPPLIES
Acrylic paint, palette, sand, paintbrush

1 Put some acrylic paint on your palette and sprinkle sand into it.

2 Use your brush to thoroughly mix the sand into the paint.

3 Brush the paint and sand mixture onto a page and allow it to dry completely.

SCRAPING

You don't always need to apply acrylic paint with a paintbrush. You can devise a variety of effects and textures by using a variety of objects. A paint scraper or palette knife is a common choice, but try using anything from your finger to a piece of cardboard to an expired plastic gift card.

SUPPLIES

Acrylic paint, palette, scraper

1 Scoop up a little acrylic paint with the scraper.

2 Spread the paint onto the page. Vary the pressure for different effects.

3 Use the tip of the knife or corner of the scraper to reveal light marks and lines.

TIP

This technique produces areas of thick paint. Allow the paint to dry completely before you turn the page or close the journal. You do not want to accidentally glue pages together with the acrylic paint.

111

STAMPING

When stamping with acrylic paint, it is very important to work quickly because the paint dries quickly. You will also need to clean off surfaces and rubber stamps with water and soap before the paint dries.

SUPPLIES
Acrylic paint, palette, object for stamping, paintbrush (optional)

1 Brush acrylic paint onto bubble wrap.

2 Press the bubble wrap onto a page and lift to reveal the stamped pattern.

3 Paint a rubber stamp with acrylic paint. Be careful not to glob the paint onto the stamp.

4 Press the stamp onto a page and lift.

IMAGE TRANSFER & ACRYLIC PAINT

With this arsenal of techniques, it is possible to construct complex and intriguing visuals in your journal. Here we use some image transfer and acrylic paint techniques to add to the example page from the previous sections. For steps one through nine, see pages 56–57 and 87.

10 Make a packaging tape transfer from a magazine image and glue it onto the page.

11 Use acrylic to paint various parts of the page. Change the opacity to allow certain elements already in place to show through.

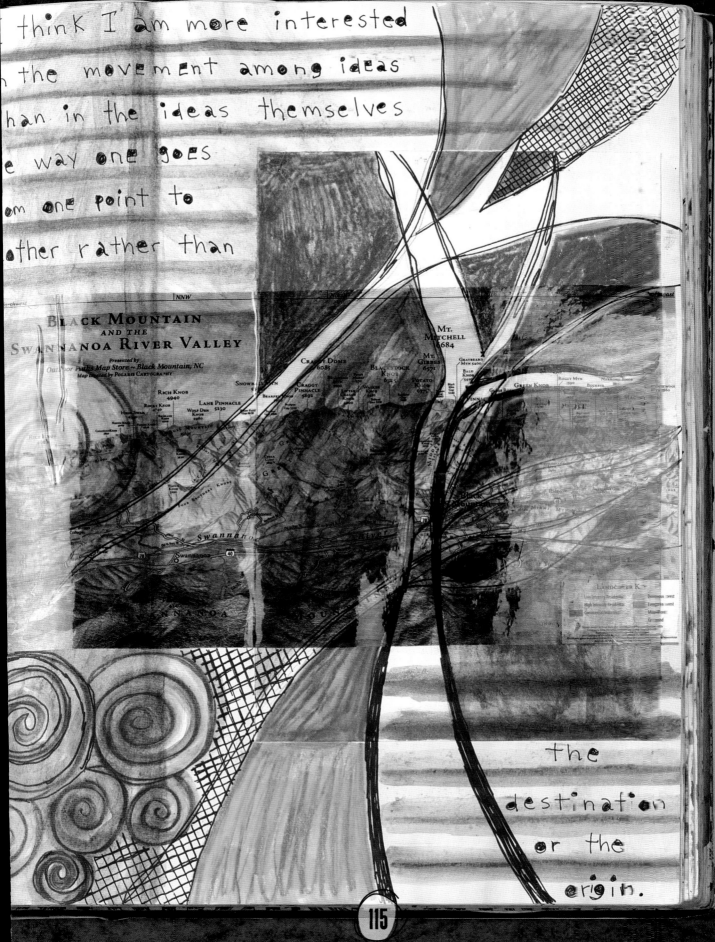

think I am more interested

the movement among ideas

han in the ideas themselves

e way one goes

m one point to

other rather than

the

destination

or the

origin.

BLACK MOUNTAIN
AND THE
SWANNANOA RIVER VALLEY

Presented by
Outdoor Trails Map Store ~ Black Mountain, NC
Map compiled by POLARIS CARTOGRAPHY

ONCE YOU ACCEPT AN IDEA IT'S AN IDEA
WHOSE TIME HAS COME.

WANTED
#06281968
DAVID R. MODLER

WANTED
#12221973
ERIC M. SCOTT

ARTISTIC ACCOMPLICES

ARTISTIC ACCOMPLICES
February 18 - March 15, 2005
Recent mixed media paintings
by David R. Modler and Eric M. Scott

Perquimans Arts League Gallery
Hertford, North Carolina

Opening Reception:
Friday, February 18, 2005 6-8pm

Most of our lives are about **proving** something to ourselves or someone else.

ART IS

I feel like I've worked through my funk — at least in regards to my art. I've been consistently working in the journal — mostly at school trying to deal with being there. Most of the time it isn't bad but, at times I don't want to be there. I've been trying to get to the things that matter the most — trying to put my life on the right path! I feel like I'm with my art. I've been able to give it more meaning by tying the layering processes I so thoroughly enjoy to memories and experiences.

When we remember something we see it through so many influences — Life is a big blur of multiple perceptions, memories, and experiences. When we think about it, it all presents itself at once.

I've found new energy to work on my art. I've discovered the path my art was already taking when I first began to experiment with layers. I enjoyed the process I did not see any big meaning behind it. Much of that early work is muddled and chaotic. I feel that I've boiled the compositions down to simpler more bare-bones ones. I feel like I know where I want my work to go. I see that some of the work was already heading in that direction — simpler compositions — simpler meanings. Consistent work makes it easier

[I] WANT TO **CONNECT** TO PEOPLE - TO [MO]VE THEM - TO LET THEMSELVES [BE] SURPRISED - TO MAKE THEM [TH]**INK**. I WANT AN ART [TH]AT WILL MAKE THE [VI]EWER TAKE NOTICE IN A [CON]TEMPLATIVE WAY. I [W]ANT THE VIEWER TO [TH]INK & WONDER WHAT [K]INDS OF THINGS HAD [G]ONE THROUGH MY [MI]ND. I WANT THEIR [G]EARS TO TURN (TO [BO]RROW THE METAPHOR)

[I] LIKE THE **INTER-**[PL]**AY** OF MAN & NATURE [IN] MY WORK WHETHER [MA]TERIAL, SYMBOLIC, [O]R ELEMENTAL. [G]EOMETRIC VS. OR-[G]ANIC. **MAN VS.** [N]**ATURE**. MECHANICAL [VS]. NATURAL THE 1ST [M]OMENT THAT I TRULY [F]ELT THAT **PUSH/PULL** WAS [IN] SCULPTURE CLASS IN [C]OLLEGE WHEN I USED [M]AN-MADE MATERIALS - [I].E. NAILS OR CANS & PLAYED [TH]EM OFF NATURAL MATERIALS - [I].E. TREE BARK. NOW THAT THEME POPS [UP] A BIT IN MY ART. TAKE MY MIXED [M]EDIA **PORTRAITS**. I BEGIN WITH A [N]ATURAL PORTRAIT DRAWN OR PAINTED - A [LI]VING, **BREATHING**, REALISTIC PORTRAIT. I [PL]AY THAT OFF AGAINST RECTANGLES, [S]TRAIGHT LINES, CIRCLES, STENCILED LETTERS. [GE]OMETRIC (MAN-MADE) VS. ORGANIC (NATURAL) [TH]OSE LINES & SHAPES POP UP. BUT OFTEN IT[S] A GEOMETRIC INTERPRETATION OF ORG[ANIC] SIMPLE, **ELEGANT** LINES ARE NOT BASED [ON] THE LINES IN A TREE OR RIVER OR INSECT

THE
GEARS
ARE
TURNING

I CAN'T SEE MYSELF MAKING MUCH ART **DEVOID** OF THE FIGURE THOUGH SOME [NON]-OBJE[CTIVE] [G]IVE [AR]... [I]S S[O]... SI[M]P[LE] [VI][S]UA[L] BEA-TIFU[L] IT LA... SOMETH... WHETHE[R] IT'S MY O[WN] WORK OR A FAMOUS ARTIST LIK[E] POLLOCK OR MONDRIAN. I AM INHER[ENT]LY DRAWN [TO] THE **FIGURE**. GUESS POLLOC[K] & MONDRIAN REMOVED T[HE] HUMANITY FR[OM] THE IMAGE BUT NOT F[ROM] THE **PROCE**[SS] BUT THAT'S A STEP [TOO] REMOVED FOR ME.

THEY ARE NATURE **STYLIZED** AND MODIFIED. THEY ARE BASED IN NATURE BUT NOT COPIES OF NATURE JUST AS THE GEOMETRIC ARE NOT COPIES OF MAN MADE OBJECTS BUT BASED ON THEM.

SHARPSHOOTING

All of the art materials and techniques we've discussed could keep you busy for quite some time creating visual pages in your journal. But the merging of the image and the word is what sets the visual journal apart from the sketchbook, the art journal and the written journal. This is where the real power of the journal lies. Images can express what words cannot. And poignant phrases and quotes can sometimes capture a moment or a feeling better than an image.

Therapists and other experts can tell you that journal writing is a meaningful way to deal with the good and bad of life. It helps people vent frustrations and disappointments, deal with trauma and loss, put things into perspective and celebrate the important things in life.

Writing can help you get over hurdles, and it can be a path to higher creativity and a better life. In our workshops and seminars, we have seen over and over again the floodgates of emotions and creativity open wide during the writing process as people tap into dormant emotions. Words and images help them deal with the flood. We have found that it is not always necessary to be able to read what you have written. Sometimes it is more important just to be caught up in the act of writing.

There are numerous techniques and ideas to consider when writing in a journal. Over the years, we have developed various methods for incorporating words into the journal and for bringing images and writing together to conceive powerful pages that speak on many levels.

DAILY JOURNAL WRITING

Many visual journalists use the visual journal like a traditional journal and write in the journal every day or nearly every day. It is easy enough to grab a pen, pencil or marker and write about what has occurred each day. Some people fill pages, and others sum up the day in a few short phrases or a couple of sentences. When combined with paint, collage and other imagery, words create a visual diary. Drawings and bits and pieces of ephemera bring daily life into the journal in a very tangible way.

The visual journal, like a traditional journal, can be a place to vent frustrations, to deal with pains and heartaches or to celebrate life's milestones. The addition of images, color and artistic techniques gives this type of journaling added power, strength and meaning. Memories are quickly sparked by a glance, giving the visual journalist instant recall of a day, a place, a person or an event. Every moment is significant at the moment it occurs. The visual journal provides a place to record the nuances of those events before they slip away and are forgotten.

By writing about your life, you begin to create a cherished artifact—something you will want to look over and savor. The visual journal is a true extension of you, and you can pour your life, your thoughts, your hopes and your fears into its pages.

You may be apprehensive about getting personal in the visual journal, fearing that someone may see it and read it. But it is your journal and your journey, and it can be as private or as public as you wish it to be. You can keep a visual journal all for yourself or you can share it with the world—so get as deep, raw and personal as you like.

STREAM-OF-CONSCIOUSNESS WRITING

Stream-of-consciousness writing has been a valuable tool for the creative writer for quite a while, and it is just as valuable for the visual journalist. In her book *The Artist's Way*, Julia Cameron discusses what she calls the "morning pages"—three pages she writes in longhand every morning. Julia refers to stream-of-consciousness writing as "brain drain" and explains that this type of writing clears the mind of clutter and makes way for creativity.

Following the lead of fellow visual journalist Jeanne Minnix, we have adapted this concept for use as a timed, seven-minute writing exercise on specific topics. The idea is to find a quiet spot, sit for one minute in silence focusing on the topic, and then write for seven uninterrupted minutes. The trick is to keep writing. If you find yourself at a point where you cannot think of anything to write, then simply write, "I cannot think of anything to write. I cannot think of anything to write," or write the prompt over and over. Continue this until the writing begins to flow again. Don't worry about spelling, punctuation, grammar or making sense. Just let the writing flow. When time is up, bring your thoughts to a close. You may want to set an audible timer so you don't have to watch the clock.

The more you do this type of writing, the more comfortable you will become with the process. Many times you will find yourself beginning with one topic and winding up writing about something completely different. This could be something that may have been bothering you but that you had not consciously admitted or spoken out loud before. The natural flow of the writing allows things like this to come out. And it is perfectly fine. Stream-of-consciousness writing lets you open up and dump the stuff that gets in the way of your creativity on a page. Writing can be a great spark for a visual journal page as you deal with issues further by adding layers of art.

When we Journal Fodder Junkies do stream-of-consciousness writing, we often make an effort to think about dualistic pairs. These are ideas and concepts that tend to have opposite meanings and associations. We will write on one topic and then a short time later—usually the same day or the next—we will write on the other. In the box, below, are some topics and dualistic pairs to think about.

You can easily come up with your own starter topics simply by writing about a pressing matter. Whatever the topic, it allows you to focus as you write, and some people say having a topic makes stream-of-consciousness writing easier for them.

The question of privacy always comes up because of the nature of stream-of-consciousness writing. Sometimes such writing will take you to a psychological or emotional place that you did not expect to go, and you may write something you wish you had not. We encourage people never to tear pages out of the journal. It is okay if the writing gets covered up or obscured by paint, collage or drawing. It is not important that others read it. It is important that you wrote it, and if it needs to be hidden, that's okay. If it's on a separate piece of paper, you can tear it up and glue it into the journal in a way that makes it impossible to read. Or perhaps you can seal it in an envelope. Some people keep a visual journal strictly for themselves and allow no one to see it. Other people have no problem baring their souls to the world. Find a balance that is comfortable for you.

After you have done some stream-of-consciousness writing, think about various ways that you can incorporate it into your journal. Try writing directly in your journal. Write on other surfaces—tracing paper, vellum, notebook paper or a paper bag—then think about how to put that into your journal. You could collage it, fold it up and put it into an envelope that has been glued in, rip it or cut it up and collage it, or perhaps sew it in. Think about highlighting key words in your writing by making them bold, a different color or rewriting them in larger letters. Also consider stenciling key words and phrases.

I BELIEVE...	I DON'T BELIEVE...
I THINK...	I FEEL...
MY DREAM...	MY NIGHTMARE...
I WANT ...	I NEED...
I LOVE...	I HATE...
I HOPE...	I FEAR...
LIGHT...	DARK ...
GOOD...	EVIL...
WORK...	PLAY...

PROMPTS

Prompts provide a mental push when you are having trouble getting started. Use any of the prompts we've shared or begin your own list of prompts. You can find many resources with suggested prompts on the Internet and in books. You can even create a prompt jar: Type or write a list of prompts, cut apart the individual items, place them in a jar and pull one out anytime you get stuck. You can also put together a prompt deck by writing prompts on index cards. Consider using key words and phrases from your own writing.

You may find that images, colors and other visual elements help you express the ideas that arise as you write. We strongly encourage you to embellish your writing visually. Also realize that text may be added to pages in progress or may be used to begin new pages. As the visual journalist, you have unlimited freedom to decide what and where.

REFLECT ON THE FOLLOWING:

Yesterday
The past week
The past month
The past year
Your greatest triumph
Your greatest tragedy
Your greatest joy
Your greatest regret
A time when you overcame adversity
A time when you performed an act
    of tolerance
A time when you experienced an act
    of tolerance
A time when you witnessed an act
    of tolerance

DOCUMENT THE FOLLOWING:

Everything that happens today
All the memorable events from yesterday
All the memorable events from the last week
All the memorable events from the last month
All the memorable events from the last year
All that you are grateful for in your life
All the things that you would change

CONTEMPLATE THE FOLLOWING QUESTIONS:

Who is your favorite artist?
Who is your favorite musician?
Who is your favorite actor?
Who is your favorite writer?
Who is your favorite athlete?
Who is your favorite politician?
Who is your favorite celebrity?
Who am I? Why?
Who do I want to be? Why?
How do others see me? Why?
What are my greatest fears?
What is one thing I would change
    about myself?
What is one thing I would change
    about the world?
What is one thing I would change
    about my life?
Where is one place I would like to go
    if I could?
Who is one person I would like to
    meet if I could?

REACT TO THE FOLLOWING WORDS:

transformation
passion
nostalgia
time
place
space
imagination
family
action
reaction
memory
recollection
power
change
resistance
struggle
solitude
sanctuary
independence
wholeness
stability
security
goals
vision
relationships
connections
growth
evolution
work
play

RESPOND TO THE FOLLOWING:

A random word out of the dictionary
A piece of music
A poem
A book or article you have recently read
A quote by a famous person
The quote: "Nothing ventured,
     nothing gained."
The quote: "The greatest risk in life is
     not taking one."
The quote: "It is what it is."
The quote: "It will be what it will be."
The quote: "Such is life."
A dream you once had
A nightmare you once had

TRY ONE OF THE FOLLOWING:

Choose a page from a newspaper. Cut
out thirty words. Arrange and assemble
these words into a short poem. Glue
this poem into your journal and react
to it.

Photocopy a page from a favorite book.
Glue the copy into your journal. Read
over the text and identify, highlight,
circle or underline one to three key
words from each line to create a
unique version of the text.

Select five images from magazines and
newspapers. Cut them out and glue
them into your journal. Respond to
the images.

Using photographs and writing,
create a timeline of your life.

Create a "bucket list"—a list of all
the things you want to do before you
die. Why haven't you done them?

WRITE LETTERS TO THE FOLLOWING:

yourself
a friend
a lover
an enemy
a stranger
a pivotal person
your parent(s)
your child(ren)

STORIES

Storytelling is an ancient art form, and the visual journal lends itself to telling stories, both fictional and true, with words and images. In the visual journal, it's easy to illustrate these stories with photographs, colors and simple imagery. The story of a person's life easily unfolds, and it is not uncommon for viewers of visual journals to feel like they know the journals' creators rather well. But the stories do not have to be personal or autobiographical. Stories of any kind are always welcome in the journal.

Just as with drawing, many people are better at telling stories than they think. Think about the stories you want to tell. You can tell your life's story with words, color and images. You can find old photographs and old bits of ephemera to help tell the story of your childhood. Make color copies of photos if you do not want to use the originals. You can tell the story of your friends and family, or you can write your own fictional stories about whatever you wish. The images that you use can be the spark for a story or the illustrations for the story. Whether you intend it or not, the visual journal tells stories of its own, and others will relish reading them.

TYPES OF FAILURE

ACCIDENT
MISTAKE
WEAKNESS
INABILITY
INCORRECT METHOD
USELESSNESS
INCOMPATIBILITY
EMBARRASSMENT
CONFUSION
REDUNDANCY
OBSOLESCENCE
INCOHERENCE
UNRECOGNIZABILITY
ABSURDITY
INVISIBILITY
IMPERMANENCE
DECAY
INSTABILITY
FORGETABILITY
TARDINESS
DISAPPEARANCE
CATASTROPHE
UNCERTAINTY
DOUBT
FEAR
DISTRACTABILITY

Emily told me today that she got several of her cousins into the journals and they in turn got several friends into them. Slowly the revolution is spreading. Paige told me that she was going into withdrawal because she had left her journal at school over the weekend. Stories like th make me aware of how powerful the journal is. As I began to retype the journal book today, I realized how excited it makes me to think that one day peopl may pick up my book and read the words and find inspiration from it the way I have found inspiration from others. I hope that the book Dave and I are putting together becomes one of those standards that visual journalists keep on their shelves. I've been throwing around the idea of the Journal Fodder Junkies as a business wit a website, books, stickers. Dave and I jol about it, but I think we both would li it to come to pass. With contacts Dave h made we are consistently doing workshops NCAT is going to fly for the 3 The Revolution Has B...

LISTS

One of the easiest ways to write in the visual journal is to incorporate lists of any kind—from to-do lists to lists of favorite things. You can easily glue lists written on separate pieces of paper, like grocery lists, into your visual journal, creating an instant record of your trip to the store. To-do lists even allow the journal to become a tool for day-to-day life.

But lists do not have to be so mundane. You can list your favorite foods, music, places, people and so on. You can list goals and dreams, and you can list all the things for which you are grateful each day. You can list the people you admire, the qualities in yourself that you most cherish or your fondest memories. You could list all the places you wish you could go and all the people you wish you could meet. You could list random words or powerful thought-provoking words. You could write top ten lists. In other words, you could fill your journal with lists. The lists you decide to include provide insight, record your day and help you dream and be grateful.

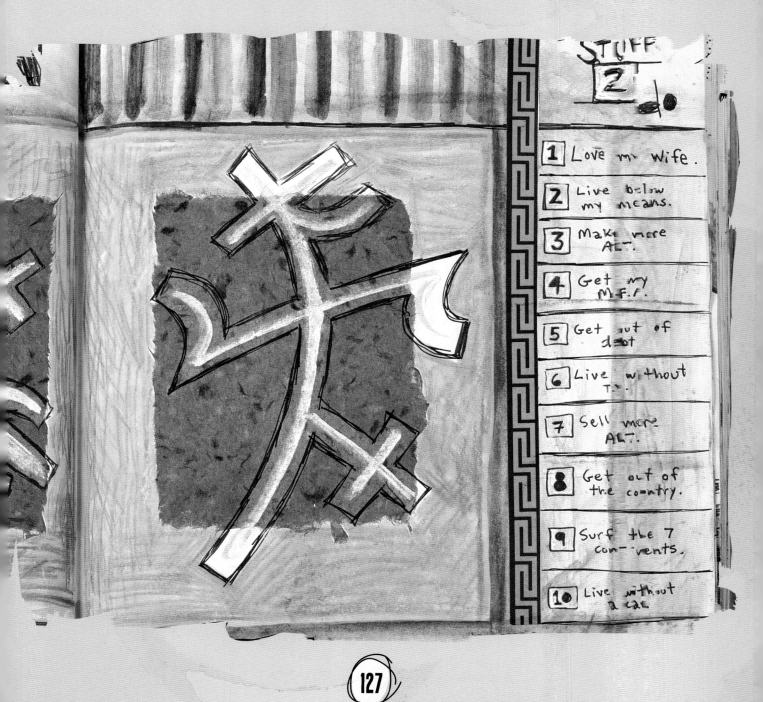

STUFF 2 do

1. Love my wife.
2. Live below my means.
3. Make more ART.
4. Get my M.F.A.
5. Get out of debt
6. Live without TV.
7. Sell more ART.
8. Get out of the country.
9. Surf the 7 con- vents.
10. Live without a car

aborate

silhouette

penetrate

capture

investigate

shudder

delicate

RANDOM WORDS

Words for the journal can come from anywhere. The juxtaposition of random words can have a strange, poetic effect. Often these words can spark incredible pages and amazing imagery. As you try some of these ideas, you will come to see the potential of the random word.

eavesdropping

Keeping a small pad on which to write is a handy way to jot down words and phrases you overhear in the course of your day. Sometimes profound morsels get spoken in ordinary conversations.

word of the day

There are many places to find words of the day. A simple search of the Internet reveals countless word-of-the-day sites. Dictionary.com, Merriam-Webster Online, and *The New York Times* all have word-of-the-day pages on their Web sites. There are even word-of-the-day calendars, the pages of which make great fodder.

magnetic poetRy

This popular word toy is an effective way to select words. The same random juxtaposition of words that has made refrigerators a source of constant entertainment works well in the visual journal. You can even glue the actual magnets into the journal.

dictionaRy

Randomly pick a word or several words from a dictionary and use them as inspiration for your journal. Surrealists often wrote poetry this way.

word bank

Devise a word bank by cutting words from newspapers and magazines and placing them in a jar. Or type and print up a list of words to cut up and place in the jar. Anytime you need inspiration, you can withdraw from your word bank.

opeRative woRds

Operative words are the words that you stress, embellish and emphasize in your writing. Look over some of your previous writings to find these words. Trust your gut reaction. Your own writing already contains many words that can spark ideas for your journal. You may want to create a list (and put it in your journal) of these random, operative words.

Reading

As you read a book, magazine or newspaper, list any words and phrases that pop out at you. You can write them directly in the journal or you may want to keep a running list in a small notebook.

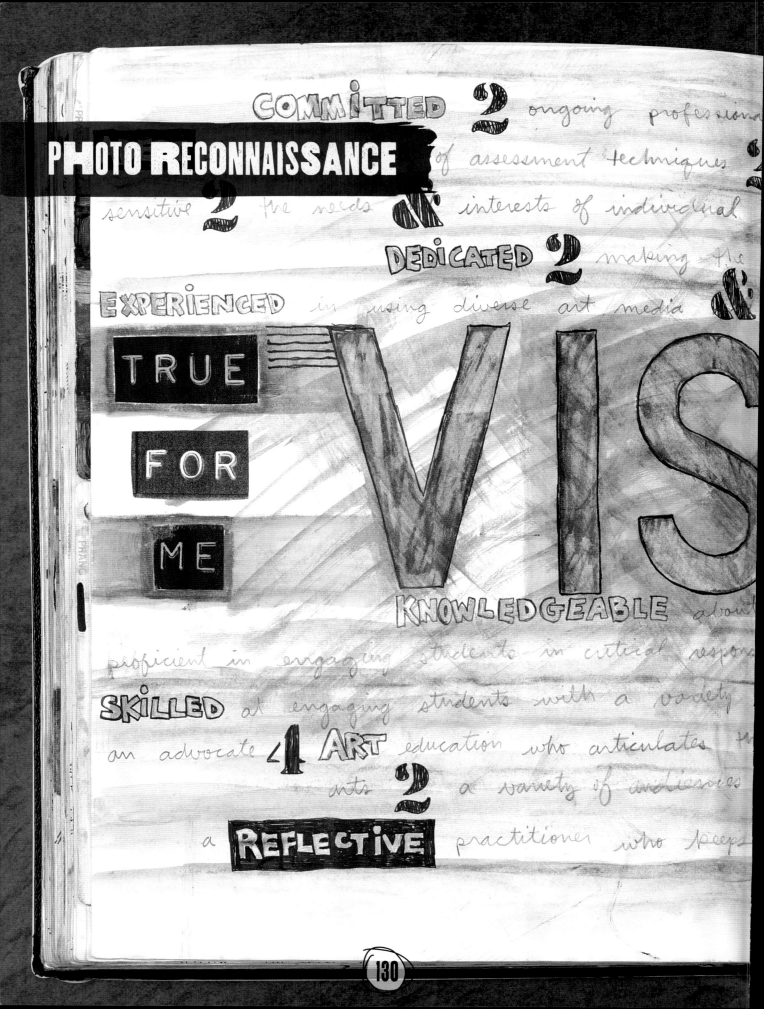

COMMITTED 2 ongoing professional

of assessment techniques

sensitive 2 the needs & interests of individual

DEDICATED 2 making the

EXPERIENCED in using diverse art media &

VIS

TRUE

FOR

ME

KNOWLEDGEABLE about

proficient in engaging students in critical respons

SKILLED at engaging students with a variety

an advocate 4 ART education who articulates

arts 2 a variety of audiences

a REFLECTIVE practitioner who keeps

DEVELOPMENT & **LEARNING**

evaluate teaching

students

visual arts accessible & meaningful 2 all students

studio **PROCESSES**

ION

TO

THE

TOP

multiple cultural art FORMS past & present

2 works of art & visual culture

learning **STYLES** in the classroom

importance of students learning in the **VISUAL**

up with the current literature & best practices

PAST ACTIONS ARE AN INDICATOR OF FUTURE ACTIONS

Portfolio option: Drawing & Design Exercises

Make a free-hand perspective drawing of one corner of a room within your dwelling. Include at least three pieces of furniture. Draw this view as realistic as possible.

Crumple an 8.5"×11" sheet of paper. Leave it crumpled and place it under a bright light. On another sheet of paper draw the crumpled sheet as realistically as possible.

Draw a geometric volume that is being vigorously by an internal force. Note: This is an exercise that requires your interpretation. You should determine what the internal force is and how it is visually affecting the geometric volume.

Select three pieces of fruit or vegetables and place them in a window sill or similar location where you can see both the fruit and vegetables and a landscape or cityscape beyond. Draw the space between. Note: In this exercise, the "space between" can be interpreted in many ~~different~~ ways. We are interested in a rich and varied visual interpretation.

Select two objects: one that is large, heavy and light in color; the other that is small, lightweight and dark. In a series of at least four drawings, transform one object into another.

Render a self portrait from observation using a mirror. When planning your drawing consider composition and the use of positive and negative space. Complete this exercise as much detail as possible.

Draw a device of your own invention that solves the last problem that you encountered.

Using a digital or analog camera provide a photographic illustration for "page 87" of your autobiography. Alternative: Do a pencil illustration of this exercise.

Arrange a still life composition consisting of at least one bell pepper and three utensils. Before rendering physically alter one or more of these objects. Using a pencil, draw your creation as realistically as possible.

Draw your hand as realistically as possible holding an object that ~~is~~ has special meaning to you.

EXPERIMENTING WITH TEXT

It is easy to get in the habit of writing in the visual journal in the same way all the time. It becomes hard to break comfortable, lazy text styles. There are many quick and simple ways to shake up your writing. Here are some of the options.

Stencils

Plastic stencils come in a variety of fonts and sizes, and you can use them with pencils, markers, paints and other media. Keep thin stencils in a pocket in the journal so they are handy and accessible. You can even create your own stencils from posterboard or flexible plastic sheets in order to have unique and personal lettering on hand at any given moment.

Stamps

You can also use rubber stamps with a variety of media from traditional stamp ink to paint. Just make certain to clean the stamps thoroughly after use to avoid damaging them. You can even carve your own stamps from old corks or rubber erasers for unique and personal lettering. Remember to reverse the letter when you carve it so it stamps in the correct orientation.

Drawn text

Draw large and dynamic letters and words into your journal. Such letters and words act as graphic devices—elements that rely on visual impact. Block and bubble letters are examples of letters that take on a graphic nature. Experiment with size, style and color as you hand draw text and words.

Printed text

Thanks to the convenience of computers and the Internet, printed text is now a common element used for embellishment. You can quickly print and glue words, quotes and other text into your journal. Your text can be relevant to the content of a page or random and oddly juxtaposed. Printed text can even be transferred using image transfer techniques.

Found text

Everything from telephone book pages to newspapers to flyers and copies can be glued into the journal. It is not necessary that the text relate to the theme or the idea of the page. It is enough that it gives the page texture and layers.

Quotes, poems and Lyrics

Meaningful quotes, poems and song lyrics are yet another source of text for your journal. The words can be printed, handwritten, drawn or transferred. Often lyrics of the songs you listen to while journaling make their way onto the page as they get into your head.

Note taking

Because the visual journal can travel with you, it is a natural place to take notes, whether as a student in a class or as a worker in a business meeting. Because of the visual nature of the journal, visual learners may even remember the notes better. If you write notes in your journal, you can still highlight key concepts and important information.

Altered books

Some people prefer to journal in an old book and will glue together pages to create thick, durable foundations. The book's preexisting text can be hidden, obscured or incorporated into the page. Using an altered book takes away the blank, white page, adding an instant first layer. It is fine to ignore the text that is there and journal right on top of it.

WRITING TOOLS

Another way to shake up your writing is to experiment with the type of writing implement you use. Try a variety of writing and drawing materials. In the examples below, water has been brushed over the water-soluble materials to give you an idea of how you can further manipulate your writing.

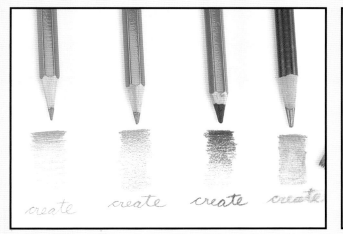

A variety of graphite pencils.

A variety of pens.

Regular and watercolor pencils.

A variety of markers.

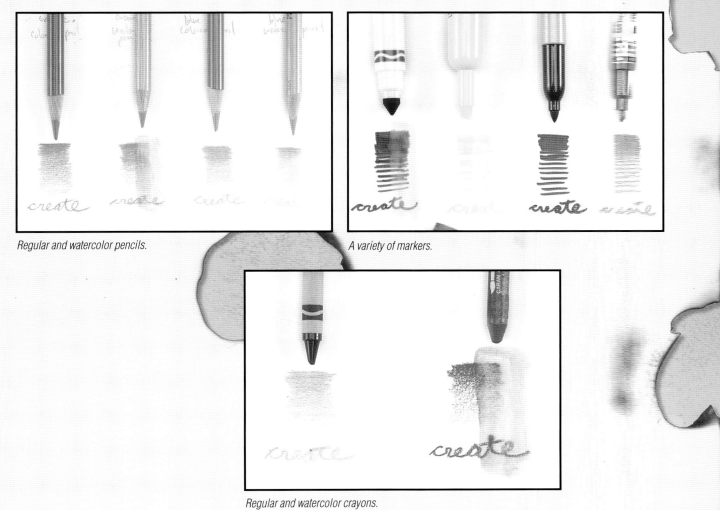

Regular and watercolor crayons.

GO GLOBAL   Gail

- Integrated Units
- novel-based instruction
- community story quilt ★ SOCIAL STUDIES
- crop growth simulation ★ SCIENCE
- Connections ★ MATH.
- internet ★ TECHNOLOGY
- writing ★ WRITING PROMPTS
- literature ★ LITERATURE CIRCLES

Melinda Avis and Mary was BE

DiFFERE
DOES DIFFER
YOGI

WHA

bauhau
philosop

From FRANKLIN.   form follows function...
function can also follow form

Cecilia
Melisa
Ann

Building Community is the Foundation

LEARNing ARMAS DEVELOPMENT
systems in place

CENTERS:
- Clay
- puppets
- reading
- sand box
- co-op learning

BECOME A CARING
COMMUNITY
OF ACTIVE LEARNERS

PINEHURST   TUGRAT = SIGNATURE

SOJOURN INTO LEARNIN

looked at writing tests
looked for trends
weaknesses
conventions

INCLUSION
all children can learn

Giftedness in POVERTY   free themselves from negative s
work and study will pa
is an attitude that gi

WRITING IN THE JOURNAL

When adding words and text to your journal, you do not have to write in your usual handwriting. Sometimes it is not even important to be able to read the text, and you can obscure it with paint, cover it up with collage or hide it in envelopes. Consider the following visual variables when you add text and writing.

Size

Large words gain visual importance and become points of emphasis. Small text becomes more of a visual texture.

Style or Font

Font variety can spice up your writing. The contrast of two different fonts allows you to draw focus and attention. Try different styles of writing or different styles of text. Find books on lettering and typography, the art of using type, in your local library and investigate the variety of fonts in the word processing program on your computer.

Color

Color goes a long way toward making a visual impact. Complementary colors such as purple and yellow or blue and orange stand out and contrast when placed next to each other. Some analogous colors, like blue and purple, are so similar they begin to blend together. Dark text will stand out on light backgrounds, whereas light colors like yellow tend to blend in. Color can also help you convey a mood. Light blues convey a sense of peace and calm, but dark blues may evoke sadness.

Direction

We often get stuck writing from left to right, but words and writing can go in any direction. You can write vertically or follow along curved lines and meander around the page. Try turning your journal in different directions as you write.

Media

You can use different writing, drawing and painting materials to jazz up text and writing. Doing so adds variety to the journal and can foster creativity as you break out of the ordinary. Experiment with a variety of pens, markers and paint.

WRITING ON ALTERNATIVE SURFACES

Writing on surfaces other than the journal page opens the door to many creative options. First you must choose the surface. You can select paper based on its color, texture and opacity. Then you must decide how to incorporate the material into the journal. You can use the writing as one large block, tear it up, cut it into strips or do anything else you can think of. Get creative.

The same text written on five pieces of vellum. Four have been embellished with a variety of media.

The text glued onto a page in a large block. The vellum allows the color and images on the page to show through.

The text cut into strips, glued to a page and embellished with watercolor paint.

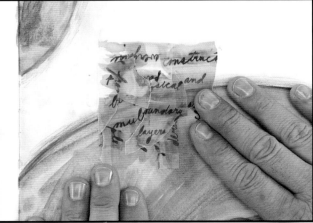

The text torn up and glued into a rectangle.

The page and text embellished with metallic marker and black ink.

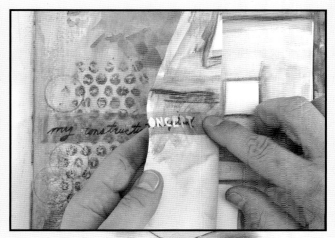

The text cut into strips and glued so it wraps around a page.

The text going across several pages.

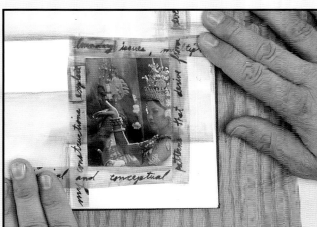

The text used to frame an image.

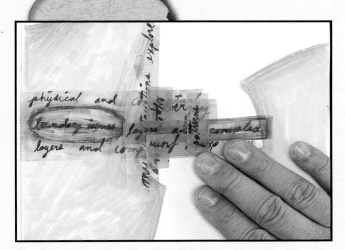

The text cut into strips and woven together.

ADDING TEXT WITH WATER-SOLUBLE MEDIA

Try using drawing media like watercolor pencil or water-soluble graphite to make the text more of a visual device. Brush water or watercolor paint over your words and allow the words to blend and bleed as much as you desire. If certain words become illegible, you can go back with other media and pull them back out. You can even highlight and embellish operative words.

SUPPLIES

Water-soluble graphite or watercolor pencil, water, paintbrush, ink pen, marker

1 Write your text with a water-soluble graphite or watercolor pencil.

2 Brush water over the text. Allow the pencil to bleed. It's okay if words disappear. You decide how legible the writing remains.

3 Allow the page to dry.

4 Use ink, marker and watercolor pencil to emphasize words. When embellishing the words, experiment with size, thickness and style.

As with any material and technique, you can use text to create more layers on a page to help further develop personal themes and impart greater meaning. Let us visit the example page one last time to add some writing to this layered page. For steps 1 through 11, see pages 56–57, 87 and 113.

12 Use a variety of pens to write in your journal.

13 A finished layered page.

WHAT ARE YOU AFRAID OF?

LIVING? DYING? LOVING? HATING? OPENING? FEELING? REFLECTING? LETTING GO? SEARCHING? BELIEVING? GROWING? FREEING YOUR MIND? SEEING? PROCRASTINATING? NOT BELIEVING? JOURNEYING? CLOSING YOUR HEART? BEING? LAGGING BEHIND? DREAMING? LEARNING? HURTING? FINDING? LOSING? MOVING AHEAD? WONDERING? HOLDING ON? CRYING? HOPING? WINNING? DARING? REACH SMILING? PRAYING? MAINTAINING? HOLDING OUT?

SHARING? DOING? HESITATING CARING? ASKING? HOLDING? RULING LAUGHING? QUESTIONING? CREATING FINDING OUT? HURRY LOOKING IN? REVEAL

WHAT SHOULD A STUDENT
GET FROM YOUR CLASS?

TRAGEDY EXTACY DOOM AND SO FORTH

Y2K5

SWIPES AND SWABS DRIPS AND DRIBBLES

HERE?

AM I LOVING MY WIFE ENOUGH?

HOW DO I MAKE ART PART OF LIFE?

WHO AM I ????

WHAT DO I NEGLECT? WHY?

what makes me happy?

NOT INSPIRATION

WHAT IS MY INSPIRATION?

MY VISION ??

what do I want from life...

DO I WASTE OPPORTUNITIES?

HOW IN MY LIFE

where am i trying to go?

WHAT DO I

WHAT DO I NEED?

HOW IN MY LIFE

GGEST DREAMS ??

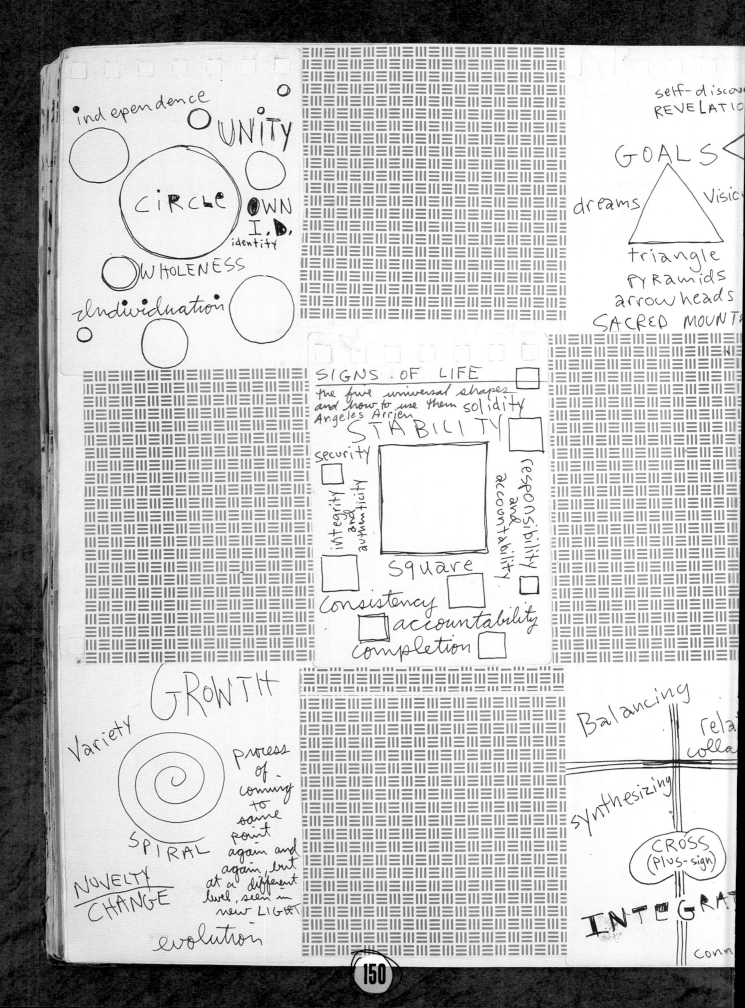

independence

○

○ UNITY

CIRCLE

OWN
I.D.
identity

○ WHOLENESS

Individuation

self-discov...
REVELATIO...

GOALS

dreams   Visio...

triangle
PYRAMIDS
arrow heads
SACRED MOUNT...

SIGNS OF LIFE
the five universal shapes
and how to use them solidity
Angeles Arrien
STABILITY

security

integrity
and
authenticity

responsibility
and
accountability

square

Consistency

accountability

completion

GROWTH

Variety

process
of
coming
to
same
point
again and
again, but
at a different
level, seen in
new LIGHT

SPIRAL

NOVELTY
CHANGE

evolution

Balancing   rela...
colla...

synthesizing

CROSS
(plus-sign)

INTEGRAT...

conn...

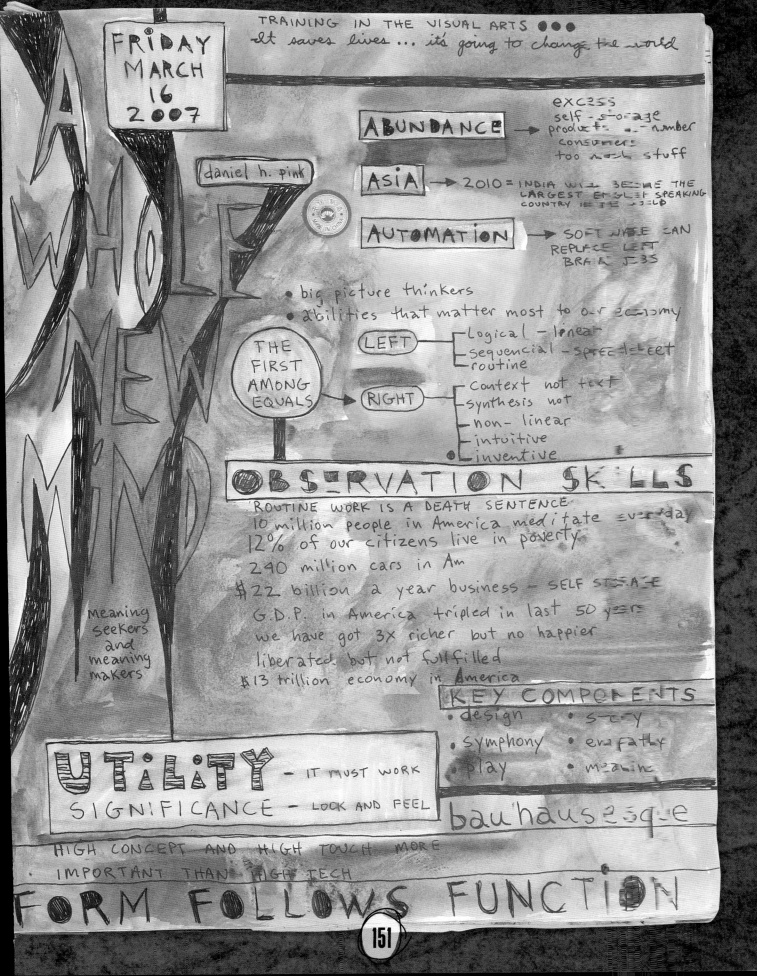

FRIDAY MARCH 16 2007

A WHOLE NEW MIND

daniel h. pink

ABUNDANCE → excess self-storage products - number consumers too much stuff

ASIA → 2010 = INDIA WILL BECOME THE LARGEST ENGLISH SPEAKING COUNTRY IN THE WORLD

AUTOMATION → SOFTWARE CAN REPLACE LEFT BRAIN JOBS

• big picture thinkers
• abilities that matter most to our economy

THE FIRST AMONG EQUALS →

LEFT ⊏ Logical - linear
Sequencial - spreadsheet
routine

RIGHT ⊏ Context not text
synthesis not
non - linear
intuitive
• inventive

OBSERVATION SKILLS

'ROUTINE WORK IS A DEATH SENTENCE
10 million people in America meditate everyday
12% of our citizens live in poverty
240 million cars in Am
$22 billion a year business - SELF STORAGE
G.D.P. in America tripled in last 50 years
we have got 3x richer but no happier
liberated but not fullfilled
$13 trillion economy in America

meaning seekers and meaning makers

KEY COMPONENTS
• design • story
• symphony • empathy
• play • meaning

UTILITY - IT MUST WORK
SIGNIFICANCE - LOOK AND FEEL

bauhausesque

HIGH CONCEPT AND HIGH TOUCH MORE IMPORTANT THAN HIGH TECH

FORM FOLLOWS FUNCTION

FINAL ORDERS

We have shared a great variety of possibilities for beginning your visual journal, and we hope that you will continue to explore your creativity. It was never our intention to lead you by the hand through the entire process, for after all, this is your journey and you must be the one who makes it. We have been here as guides, hopefully, supplying you with the ammunition you will need to continue. If you ever get bogged down or lost along the way, this book and these ideas will always be here for you. We hope that the mounds of fodder have begun to accumulate, that you are looking at the world differently and that you will continue the adventure that is the visual journal. As you go out into the world of visual journals armed with the techniques you have learned, remember that you are not alone in your pursuit.

study
research
examine
inquire

ARTISTIC ACCOMPLICES

It is hard to keep up with something when you try doing it all on your own—think about all those New Year's resolutions that go by the wayside because you don't have the support and the encouragement needed to sustain them. That's why it's important to find artistic accomplices and creative collaborators that will help you stay focused and working in the journal. We (Eric and David) have been each other's greatest allies, critics and fans these last eleven years. It has been that support and friendship that has brought about the entire Journal Fodder Junkie endeavor. Find a friend or a group of friends that will help you maintain your dedication. These friendships can sustain you through dry spells and encourage you along the way. You may find that as you keep a journal, many others become inspired by your lead. They may even ask you for tips on how they can begin, and you will be there to help them. If your friends and family are not interested, find a group or a blog online that allows you to share in the virtual world, or start your own. Many people share their visual journals on blogs and photo-sharing sites like Flickr and Photobucket. There are other Journal Fodder Junkies out there—you simply have to search for them.

A BASIC COMMITMENT

Over and over again we hear one question from curious folks: "How do you find the time to keep a visual journal?" Our response is usually: "How do you not?" Keeping a visual journal does take dedication, but once you begin, it is easy to get addicted. As mentioned at the beginning of this book, it is not that we have hours upon hours of free and uninterrupted time. Rather, we have five minutes here and ten minutes there, and that time adds up over the course of a day or week. But there is a basic commitment to using the journal, and part of that commitment is to take the journal nearly everywhere we go. We often work in it while teaching, watching TV, traveling or just waiting around. As mentioned above, it is easier to stay committed to the visual journal if you have an accomplice who will push you, prod you and inspire you.

Now it is time to truly begin the journey of your own making. Look back over the ideas we have shared. Use the ones that make the most sense to you, reject the ones that do not and find others out in the world. Open up your journal and begin creating your legacy and cultivating your creativity.

ABOUT THE AUTHORS

The visual journal has become a major force in Dave's and Eric's personal growth and creative development since they came to it about eleven years ago. Both Dave and Eric use the visual journal format extensively. In 2005, they teamed up to become the Journal Fodder Junkies. As the Journal Fodder Junkies, Dave and Eric have implemented a variety of workshops that teach the ways of the journal to all who seek its creative power. The Journal Fodder Junkies have provided formal and informal presentations at the North Carolina Art Education Association, the Virginia Art Education Association and the National Art Education Association's annual conferences and conventions. Since 2006, they have presented a week-long seminar each year at the North Carolina Center for the Advancement of Teaching

(NCCAT) on the visual journal. In addition, Dave and Eric have presented visual journals to art classes at George Mason, James Madison and Appalachian State universities, including the Content Teaching Academy at JMU in the summer of 2007. They have provided several weekend seminars and workshops for local schools and arts councils as well. Most recently the Journal Fodder Junkies presented at the 2009 National Art Education Association Convention in Minneapolis, Minnesota, and served on a panel of visiting artist-educators sharing their experiences with a graduate class at the Maryland Institute College of Art.

Eric M. Scott is an artist-educator born and raised in Washington, Pennsylvania. He earned his bachelor of science in art education from Edinboro University of Pennsylvania and currently lives with his wife in Purcellville, Virginia, where he teaches art at the high school level.

● ● ● ● ● ● ● ● ● ● ● ● ● ● ●

David R. Modler is an artist-educator who was born and raised in Baltimore, Maryland. He earned his bachelor of science and master of education degrees in art education from Towson State University in Towson, Maryland. He also has earned his master of fine arts from James Madison University in Harrisonburg, Virginia. With eighteen years of art education experience at all levels, David's focus has recently shifted to teaching in the art department at Appalachian State University in Boone, North Carolina.

Eric

David

More and more visual journal resources pop up every day, from books to Internet sites. These resources can give you new ideas and techniques to try. They offer inspiration as well as motivation when you are stagnant or blocked. Here is a list of resources that we have found especially helpful in our pursuit of the visual journal over the years. As for art supplies, we don't have many specific brand recommendations. However, we do like to work in Cachet Classic Hardbound Sketchbooks (11" x 14")—just remember, this is personal preference. Use whatever works for you.

FURTHER READING

books

Arrien, Angeles. *Signs of Life: The Five Universal Shapes and How to Use Them.* New York: Jeremey P. Tarcher/Putnam, 1998.

Beam, Mary Todd. *Celebrate Your Creative Self: More than 25 Exercises to Unleash the Artist Within.* Cincinnati, Ohio: North Light Books, 2001.

Cameron, Julia. *The Artist's Way: A Spiritual Path to Higher Creativity.* New York: Jeremy P. Tarcher/Putnam, 1992.

Carter, David A., and James Diaz. *Elements of Pop-Up: A Pop-Up Book for Aspiring Paper Engineers.* New York: Little Simon, 1999.

Diehn, Gwen. *The Decorated Journal: Creating Beautifully Expressive Journal Pages.* New York: Lark Books, 2005.

Diehn, Gwen. *The Decorated Page: Journals, Scrapbooks & Albums Made Simply Beautiful.* New York: Lark Books, 2002.

Edwards, Betty. *Drawing on the Right Side of the Brain.* Los Angeles: Jeremy P. Tarcher/Putnam, 1989.

Eldon, Kathy. *The Journey Is the Destination: The Journals of Dan Eldon.* San Francisco: Chronicle Books, 1997.

Harrison, Sabrina Ward. *Brave on the Rocks: If You Don't Go, You Don't See.* New York: Villiard Books, an imprint of Random House, 2001.

Harrison, Sabrina Ward. *Messy Thrilling Life: The Art of Figuring Out How to Live.* New York: Villiard Books, 2004.

Harrison, Sabrina Ward. *Spilling Open: The Art of Becoming Yourself.* New York: Villiard Books, 1999.

Kahlo, Frida. *The Diary of Frida Kahlo: An Intimate Self-Portrait.* New York: Harry N. Abrams Inc., 1995.

Kaupelis, Robert. *Experimental Drawing.* New York: Watson-Guptill Publications, 1980.

LaPlantz, Shereen. *Cover to Cover: Creative Techniques For Making Beautiful Books, Journals & Albums.* New York: Sterling Publishing, 1995.

Leland, Nita. *The Creative Artist: A Fine Artist's Guide to Expanding Your Creativity and Achieving Your Artistic Potential.* Cincinnati, Ohio: North Light Books, 1990.

New, Jennifer. *Dan Eldon: The Art of Life.* San Francisco: Chronicle Books, 2001.

New, Jennifer. *Drawing from Life: The Journal as Art.* New York: Princeton Architectural Press, 2005.

Perrella, Lynne. *Artists' Journals and Sketchbooks: Exploring and Creating Personal Pages.* Gloucester, Massachusetts: Quarry Books, 2004.

Zöllner, Frank. *Leonardo da Vinci: 1452-1519: Complete Paintings and Drawings.* Los Angeles: Taschen, 2003.

web sites

Creative Visions Foundation
www.daneldon.org
This is the Creative Visions Web site that tells the story of Dan Eldon and shares many pages from his journal and many of his photographs.

www.sketchbob.com
This is the Web site of artist Bob Fisher that contains many pages from his journals.

www.teeshamoore.com
This is the site of artist Teesha Moore who shares pages from her journals.

www.johncopeland.com
This is the site of artist John Copeland that shares pages from his journals.

Zettiology
www.zettiology.com
This is the site of artist Tracy V. Moore, husband of Teesha, containing pages from his journals.

The 1000 Journals Project
www.1000journals.com
This is a site administered by a man who sent one thousand journals into the world as an experiment to be passed person to person. The site has scans of pages from many of these journals.

www.1001journals.com
This is an offshoot website of the 1000 Journals Project. This site hosts a community of journal keepers who post pages from personal time and place journals.

www.visualjournaling.com
This is a site by Michael Bell, an artist and educator in the Baltimore area who shares images and ideas on visual journaling.

Live Your Creative Vision
www.kporterfield.com
This is a site by Marie Porter who contains many articles on art, journals and creativity.

Aisling Artists Journals
www.artsjournals.com
This is a site for Aisling D'Art that contains articles, information and examples of journals.

INDEX

CONTINUE YOUR JOURNEY WITH ANOTHER FINE NORTH LIGHT TITLE.

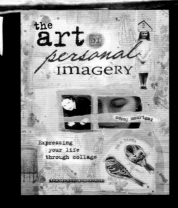

The Art of Personal Imagery by Corey Moortgat

The Art of Personal Imagery offers a new approach to collage that blends traditional collage techniques with methods of chronicling life events. The result is innovative, fresh and meaningful collage that uses modern photos, vintage images and personal writing to commemorate everything from special occasions to extraordinary every days. With step-by-step instructions and photos that illustrate countless techniques and nine intensive projects, Corey Moortgat teaches you the secrets behind the distinctive multilayered look of her collage. Achieve your own trademark style; explore ways to incorporate modern photos, mementos and journaling into your work; and discover your own personal symbols and icons!

paperback; 8.5" × 11"; 128 pages; ISBN-10: 1-58180-990-5; ISBN-13: 978-1-58180-990-9; SRN: Z0937

Creative Awakenings by Sheri Gaynor

What if you could unlatch the doors to your heart and allow yourself to explore hopes and dreams that you haven't visited for a very long time? *Creative Awakenings* is the key to opening those doors. It shows you how to use art-making to set your intentions. Creativity coach Sheri Gaynor will be your guide through the mileposts of this exciting journey. You'll learn how to create your own Book-of-Dreams Journal and a variety of mixed-media techniques to use within it. A tear-out Transformation Deck will aid you in setting your intentions. You'll also get inspiration from twelve artists who share their own experiences and artwork created with the Art of Intention process.

paperback; 8.25" × 10 ; 152 pages; ISBN-10: 1-60061-115-X; ISBN-13: 978-1-60061-115-5; SRN: Z2122

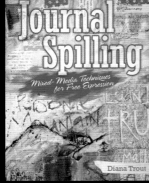

Journal Spilling by Diana Trout

Have you been waiting for someone to give you the right push to get making art in your journal? Diana Trout is the good friend you've been waiting for. In the pages of *Journal Spilling*, you will learn many new, cool mixed-media techniques, but the biggest surprise may be what you learn about yourself. There are no lines to stay inside of here. You're free to quiet your inner critic and spill color (as well as your thoughts) all over the page. Open up and see how safe of a place your private journal can truly be.

paperback; 8.25" × 10.875"; 128 pages; ISBN-10: 1-60061-319-5; ISBN-13: 978-1-60061-319-7; SRN: Z2926

Wide Open by Randi Feuerhelm-Watts

Open yourself up to a whole new way of looking at yourself, your world and your art journaling. The *Wide Open* book and deck set is all about challenging yourself to take your art to the next level. The set includes fifty idea cards featuring mixed-media artist Randi Feuerhelm-Watts's art on one side and thought-provoking instruction on the other, plus a journal for recording your ideas and artwork.

book & card kit; 6.5" × 7.5" × 1.25"; 64 pages; ISBN-10: 1-58180-911-5; ISBN-13: 978-1-58180-911-4; SRN: Z0653

These and other fine North Light titles are available at your local craft retailer, bookstore or online supplier, or visit our Web site at www.mycraftivitystore.com.